LEAVEN FOR OUR LIVES

LEAVEN FOR OUR LIVES

*conversations about bread,
faith, and companionship,
with recipes*

ALICE L. DOWNS

COWLEY PUBLICATIONS
Cambridge, Massachusetts

Published in the United States of America by Cowley Publications, a division of the Society of Saint John the Evangelist. No portion of this book may be reproduced, stored in or introduced into a retrieval system, or transmitted; in any form or by any means—including photocopying—without the prior written permission of Cowley Publications, except in the case of brief quotations embedded in critical articles and reviews.

Library of Congress Cataloging-in-Publication Data:
Downs, Alice L., 1952–
    Leaven for our lives : conversations about bread, faith, and companionship, with recipes / Alice L. Downs.
        p.   cm
Includes biographical references and index.
    ISBN 1–56101–205–X (pbk. : alk. paper)
    1. Cookery (Bread).   2. Bread—Religious aspects—Christianity.   I. Title.
TX769 .D69 2002
641.8'15—dc21
                                        2002013461

Scripture quotations are taken from *The New Revised Standard Version* of the Bible, © 1989, by the Division of Christian Education of the National Council of the Churches of Christ in the United States of America. Used by permission.

Cover photograph: Gary-Andrew Smith. Used by permission.
Cover design: Jennifer Hopcroft

This book was printed in the United States of America on acid-free paper.

Cowley Publications
907 Massachusetts Avenue
Cambridge, Massachusetts 02139
800–225–1534   •   www.cowley.org

To My Parents
Marguerite and Norton
(1916-1997) (1918-1985)

Take a farewell look
at the waves and sky.
Take a farewell sniff
of the salty sea.
A little bit sad
about the place you are leaving,
A little bit glad
about the place you are going.

from *A Time of Wonder*
by Robert McCloskey

Be gentle
When you touch bread.
Let it not lie
Uncared for—unwanted.
So often
Bread is taken for granted.

There is so much beauty
In bread.

Beauty of sun and soil.
Beauty of patient toil.
Winds and rain
Have caressed it
Christ so often blessed it.

Be gentle
When you touch bread.

—Old Scottish Verse

I would like to thank Andrea Monetti, Erin Downs Wilson and Alan Gibson for testing the recipes in this book. Their comments and suggestions have prevented glaring errors from making their way into print. I am also thankful to all the people who have attended retreats on the spirituality of baking bread. Their eagerness to seek God in hidden places has both delighted and encouraged me. Daniel Leader and David Norman, formerly of The French Culinary Institute, are two of the best teachers I have ever had. I am particularly grateful to David Norman for his formula for *levain* which I have modified for the home baker and have included in Chapter 3.

The enthusiasm of Cynthia Shattuck and the Editorial Board of Cowley Publications for this book heartened me more than they will ever know, and I am in their debt. I was blessed to have May Daw as editor. With tender mercy, she guided this work through the most arduous stages. And finally, I am so grateful to Dean, Craig and Eric: they have eaten enough bread over the years to turn into veritable doughboys. They are this baker's muse.

ACKNOWLEDGMENTS

CONTENTS

CONTENTS

Come. Join me in my comfortable kitchen. I'm baking bread today. While the dough rises, there will be time for us to talk. I'd like you to be my companion today, a *com-panion* in the original sense of the word: someone who breaks bread with me.

While the bread rises, we can talk about our lives. Like me, you are seeking companionship on your journey—especially in your journey of faith. You believe deeply in God, in God's goodness and mercy, and you are seeking the reality of God in the world around you. Perhaps you worship in community every weekend, or perhaps you find yourself on the edges of a church, wishing you were more committed but at the same time drawing back from that commitment.

All of us experience God in ways significant to our most private selves—some in great cathedrals, some in front of an easel, some in early morning silence. I, too, have searched for signs of God's presence in the familiar surroundings of my daily life. And there I have discovered how God is present to us in the most ordinary things, even in something as ordinary as a loaf of bread. Come. Let me show you this truth: where a loaf of bread is made and broken, that is where we find God.

I invite you to make the breads I describe in the pages that follow. But even if you don't use these recipes, be my companion on a journey into the ordinary stuff of life. You will soon realize that a loaf of bread is truly extraordinary.

Bread is my vehicle—my symbol, my icon—in an intuitive wandering and reflecting on God's presence in the most ordinary parts of my life. I bake bread every week, and each week the truths I have discovered are confirmed for me. I am able to see bread as a symbol of God's presence and loving abundance. For me, it is also a symbol of the fertility of the earth and the goodness arising from creation. As an image of the fullness of God's creation, it reveals a promise of trust, hope, forgiveness, and redemption. Bread is my icon, my tool for seeing beyond the commonplace into life's mysteries.

The time I spend baking bread has become a time for me to see the beauty and hope in chaos. When I bake, I am certain to make a mess, to have flour up to my elbows and dough turning to paste on the hairs of my arms. Yet baking is also about precision: the grams and ounces that keep me grounded. Baking a loaf of bread is esoteric and mundane. It is divine, and it is earthy. It is eternal, and it will turn to dust.

Baking bread is also about companionship. My niece and I live thousands of miles apart, but once long ago, I taught her to how to bake bread. She says that even now whenever she bakes, she begins by making a pot of tea to soothe the stresses from the corners of her mind. Then, as the process of baking unfolds, she thinks about the life we two have shared. This is her time to be with me.

When any of us break bread, we tenderly offer one another the gift of the earth and sky and the gift of God's very own self. Whether we are at our tables, on a picnic on the beach, or in a soup kitchen, we open ourselves to acknowledging our companionship: it takes at least two people to break bread together. Wherever you are when you break bread, look for the truth of God beyond that simple action. Seek the sacred love that surrounds you. And let the stories that follow reach the part of you that yearns to "seek the Lord while he wills to be found" (Is. 55.6).

It is for these reasons that I have written this book. I want you to search out the icon through which you see the promises of God made real and personal for you. And I want you to make excellent bread!

To bake bread, you need very few kitchen tools: a bowl, a loaf pan, a knife. But with a few more tools baking will be easier and more fun. I want you to be successful, so I am recommending a few special tools. Once you have them, you may find that they will be very handy in preparing other recipes as well.

The first tool I recommend is a kitchen scale for measuring ingredients by weight rather than by volume. Most professional bakers measure ingredients by weight in grams, using the metric system. I have a low-end battery-operated scale that I find invaluable. If you don't have a scale, don't worry. I have given all the measurements for the recipes in this book in cups as well as in grams.

I also recommend purchasing a baking stone,* sometimes sold as a pizza stone, and a baker's peel,* an implement which resembles a very large spatula. My baking stone stays permanently in the oven. If I want to protect the stone when I am baking something else, I simply cover it with aluminum foil. Otherwise, it stays in the oven, helping to heat the oven evenly. Free-form loaves bake directly on the stone, rather than on an oven rack.

The bread recipes in this book may be baked in standard nine-by-five-inch loaf pans. If you want to buy new loaf pans, buy very strong professional ones; they are worth the extra money. Another way to prepare loaves is to let them rise in willow baskets.*

*See the Glossary on page 91 for more information about the technical vocabulary of baking. Other terms are indicated in the text with an asterisk.

After the final rising in a willow basket, the dough is turned onto a baker's peel and slid into the oven to bake directly on a hot baking stone. This technique gives the finished loaf a wonderful, *artisanal*,* free-form look.

Finally, there is the question of how to mix the dough. I use a heavy-duty electric mixer for most breads. The dough hook on the mixer kneads the dough so that hand kneading is not required. I realize that most home bakers do not own heavy-duty mixers, but I have grown so attached to mine that if there were a fire, I think it would be the first thing I would save.

However, the most important "tool" to bring to your bread baking is a sense of awe. You need to know that when you bake, you are in partnership with bakers throughout time, across millennia. Furthermore, you need to be aware that you are helping to bring God's love to a hungry world by means of the fruits of creation. *For their hunger you gave them bread from heaven.* (Neh. 9:15) Let your life be leavened by God's love. Then, leaven the lives of others.

CHAPTER ONE

Stop by a bakery on your way home tonight and buy a loaf of *artisanal** bread. Choose your loaf carefully. Consider the color and appearance of the crust. You want it to be dark and firm. It should be thick and textured. The crust is the part of the bread that entices you, the part you will remember. Yet bread has two natures: one hard, one soft. The hard crust encases the crumb,* the soft, moist interior of the loaf. Even though crust and crumb are made of the same basic ingredients, they develop different natures because of their different exposures to air, heat and moisture.

Before dinner, preheat your oven to 400° Fahrenheit, wrap the bread in aluminum foil, and bake for twenty minutes. The crust will crackle and be messy, but it will have protected the crumb and kept it moist. Take a bite. The mingling of the crust and crumb—the hard and the soft—is a delight to the palate. This bread discloses its earthy origins and hints at intimate contact with the one who baked it.

THE BASIC INGREDIENTS

Bread begins with flour. Take a sack of flour and plunge your hand into it. Take time to feel the silky texture of the wheat, as cool and restful as hope. When I close my eyes, I imagine acres of wheat fields under an endless sky with clouds piled high on top of one another. In my mind, I see these clouds breaking open, pouring cooling rain on a steamy, hot, and thirsty field. Hundreds of miles away, rain falls on my face, causing me to run

LOOKING AT THE LOAF

1

inside and tear from room to room slamming windows shut. The rain that sends me indoors is the same rain that nourishes the crops and brings forth food from the earth.

But in winter, in the warmth and snugness of my kitchen, I close my eyes and imagine acres of wheat seeds hidden in the earth, blanketed by snow, waiting for their time to germinate. The winter wheat is milled especially for bread flour. Its high gluten* content produces dough that is elastic, strong, and flavorful.

Plunge your hand into a sack of flour and bring out a handful of sun and soil and snow, with particles so fine, it would be easier to count the single grains in a handful of sand. But don't be carried away by your romantic imagination. One false move and you have a mess that can take forever to clean up.

If you plunge your hands too quickly into a sack of flour, flour will fly out onto your counter top, and you'll know immediately why bakers' jackets have short sleeves, unlike the traditional long-sleeved jackets chefs wear. Bakers spend their days up to their elbows, and beyond, in flour and dough. Some of the best doughs can be incredibly sticky. And even the tidiest baker will find bits of flour everywhere: caked underneath the faucet, loose and gritty on cookbook pages, hardened in the sink, ruining sponges (oh, the sponges I have had to throw away!), accumulating little piles in every corner. One instructor at the French Culinary Institute continually chided us to keep our flour in the dough and off the floor. I seem never to have learned that lesson.

The intimate contact between the baker and the baker's craft involves far more than the touch of hands to flour. It encompasses the baker's whole body, from the shoulders to the small of the back and the arches of the feet. Dough can be heavy, and the hours one dedicates to baking can be long. And it is hot. It is always hot. At cooking school we had twelve ovens that were turned on at 8:30 in the morning and left on until 4:00 in the afternoon. At home, when I preheat the oven to 460° F and bake three loaves in succession, my oven is on for four hours. Baking is a sweaty art.

To find relief from the heat, think of the next elemental ingredient in a loaf of bread: cool, refreshing water. Its role is to moisten the flour and activate the gluten that gives the dough its structure and elasticity. Most recipes call for heating the water, but I choose to use water that is cool or near room temperature. As the water becomes incorporated into the flour, it forms a sticky mud that adheres to my fingernails, the skin of my arms, and my rings, which once again, I have forgotten to remove. I use water that has been filtered or spring water, that brings to mind the water's origins and the long-lost purity of the earth. It is deeply important to me to take time to imagine the pure origins of each of the ingredients I bring together as I bake.

Yeast is the next earthy element to be included in bread. Yeast consists largely of cells of a fungus that can be harvested from the air, grown from organic grapes left to soak in a mixture of flour and water, or cultivated from the flour and water themselves. Flour contains just enough natural simple sugar to support the fermentation process that gives dough its lift and flavor. Dough, while it is rising, is alive with yeast. Do you smell it? You should be able to sniff just a hint of decay, the catalyst of a new creation.

Salt, when used in the right amount, gives this lively dough greater form and depth of flavor. On the other hand, too much salt can kill the yeast before it has leavened the dough. In my continuing search for wholesome and natural ingredients, I choose to use salt that has been gathered from the western seacoast of Europe—from France and Portugal. I first found this sea salt in a large grocery store in Portugal. It's my habit to explore local grocery stores whenever I travel, to discover what people buy for their own kitchens, rather than what is sold for tourists. On one particular trip, I found the baking ingredients after passing by a beer bar, three-foot stacks of dried cod, a forest of sausages, olive oil, and a display of lawn chairs. After doing the currency conversion in my head, I was amazed to find that a one-kilo bag of sea salt would cost me only twenty-one cents. So while others brought home pottery, lace, and port by which to remember their trip to Portugal, I brought home bags of salt! Each week as I incorporate this salt into the water, flour, and yeast, I remember watching as it was being harvested from the Atlantic shore and dried by the sun and wind.

THE RISING DOUGH

We leave the dough alone for a while now. When we get back to it later, it is still sticky and young, but it has changed. Take a close look at its height; smell its depth. Now I spread flour onto my counter and pour out this messy living dough. With both hands, I flatten it gently to press out all the bubbles of gas. I add flour once and then again as I battle against the stickiness. Although this is grown-ups' work, if I listen intently, I imagine my mother's voice telling me once again *not* to play in the mud.

I transfer the dough back into the bowl for another rising. After that I will form it into loaves. At each stage, the dough becomes easier to handle. We can begin to sense the finished product that will emerge from the raw ingredients and from this process: real bread that may be touched, smelled, shared, and eaten. The bread's aroma intensifies, filling the kitchen and spreading throughout the house as each loaf bakes and the kitchen gets hotter. The quality of this aroma is different from that of flowers or perfume, which you must smell over and over to stay within its spell. The smell of baking bread is something palpable—part of the atmosphere. It is dense enough to support hopes and dreams. Take time to breathe, walk, and live within its enticing power.

USING ALL THE SENSES

When you take a finished loaf from the oven, examine it with all your senses. Listen to the sound of the crackling crust. Put your ear to it. Touch it. Cut a slice with a sharp knife. Take the slice and examine at it closely. Look at the holes, which should be, as an instructor of mine once said, "evenly uneven." These holes show where the yeast had been creating gas. They create more than emptiness or absence; they give the loaf lift and body. Pull the slice apart. Taste the crust and the crumb, both separately and together. The crust is chewy, completely different from the crust on lifeless store-bought bread. This crust is not going to be trimmed off anybody's peanut butter and jelly sandwich. The crumb is moist and soft, but it is strong and hearty enough to absorb olive oil or melting butter.

A loaf of artisanal bread is a harvest of the sea and the sky and the earth. Though newly created, the loaf is formed from elements as old as creation itself. For millennia, loaves like the one we've just baked have filled kitchens with their distinctive aroma. This is our contemporary loaf—neither elegant nor refined—but substantial enough to serve as nourishment for bodies and souls.

CHAPTER TWO

I am going to teach you how to bake a basic loaf of yeast bread. After this one lesson, you should be confident enough to expect good results on your second try. If you begin baking once a week, you will soon have the courage to experiment. Remember: a loaf that is less than perfect may still be fine for toast, croutons, or for feeding birds and ducks. A loaf that can feed and nourish some other living thing cannot be bad.

ASSEMBLING THE INGREDIENTS

First, make sure that you have enough flour on hand. You don't want to be caught short. You will need some type of all-purpose flour. Do not use self-rising. I use King Arthur Flour, a mixture of hard winter and spring wheats with no chemicals added. Any all-purpose flour will do, but don't use cake flour: it does not contain enough gluten to form an elastic dough.

Now make sure that you have enough of the water you intend to use. I start my bread-baking by filling up the well of my filter pitcher so that there will be plenty of filtered water by the time I need it. Generally, I use water that is near room temperature. I don't worry too much about the temperature of my ingredients.

A LESSON IN BAKING BREAD

I buy good-quality yeast whose freshness I trust. Because cake yeast has quite a short active life, I recommend using instant dry yeast, which keeps quite well for a long time in an airtight container in the freezer. Many bread recipes call for "proofing" dry yeast: dissolving it in warm water to see whether bubbles form. You don't need to do that. Simply place the required amount of yeast in the mixing bowl with the flour and water.

Use sea salt if you can: it really does have a more complex flavor than table salt. But table salt will do. Combine the flour, water, and yeast in your mixing bowl. When those ingredients are just incorporated, add the salt. Because it is very easy to forget the salt, I always put the container right in my line of vision.

I've compiled a list of bread-baking hints that you may find quite helpful. I refer to these in each recipe, but I suggest that you read them once before you even start to bake. They are found on pages 93 and 94.

Basic Yeast Bread
(Yield: two loaves)

530 grams (4 cups) flour

350 grams (1½ cups) water

2 teaspoons yeast

1½ teaspoons salt

Additional flour for kneading

Combine flour, water, and yeast in a big bowl and mix with a wooden spoon. If you use a heavy-duty mixer, attach the dough hook and use the lowest speed to mix the flour, water, and yeast. When these ingredients are mixed and the dough is still lumpy, add the salt. By hand, continue to mix for just one minute more; if you are using a mixer, continue to mix for about ten seconds.

If you are mixing by hand, dust part of your counter top with flour and turn the dough onto the floured surface. Place a pile of extra flour nearby. Begin kneading your dough. At this stage, the dough is sticky and messy. Sprinkle a little bit of flour onto the dough and fold it over itself, as though you were folding a piece of paper in half. Press the top and bottom together with the heel of your hand. Rotate the dough a quarter turn, from noon to three o'clock. Repeat this motion—always folding from the top and adding more flour as necessary—until the dough becomes smooth and elastic. This will take from five to eight minutes. Don't worry if it takes longer: you're still learning.

If you are using a mixer, ignore the instructions for kneading by hand. Instead, turn the mixer to Speed 2 and use the dough hook to process the dough for another four or five minutes. The finished dough should be smooth and pull away from the side of the bowl.

Dust the mixing bowl with a bit of flour and return the ball of dough to the bowl. Prepare a draft-free place for the dough to rise. Many bakers use a microwave oven. To add humidity that enhances rising, I suggest boiling a cup of water in the microwave and allowing the cup to remain there with the door closed. Put the uncovered bowl in the microwave with the cup of hot water and close the door. If you choose to have your dough rise elsewhere in the kitchen, you'll need to cover the bowl with a damp towel. Soak a tea towel in hot water and wring it out well. Cover the mixing bowl with the hot, damp towel and set it in the draft-free place you have chosen. Come back in an hour.

At the end of the hour, dust your work surface lightly with flour and turn the dough onto it. Do not punch the dough down; simply press it gently. Feel the air being released. Fold the dough in the following manner: Bring the top over to the middle and press. Bring the bottom to the middle and press. Bring each side over into the middle and press, first one side and then the other. Fold the whole thing once more in half and press. This degassing* process spreads the yeast throughout the dough, allowing it to make contact with new nourishment.

It is now time for the second rising. Refresh the humidity, either by boiling the cup of water in the microwave or by moistening the tea towel in hot water again. Return the dough to the bowl and set it in the same draft-free place. Come back in about forty-five minutes; the second rising takes less time.

After the second rising, prepare two nine-by-five-inch loaf pans by greasing them lightly with olive oil or vegetable oil. Cut the dough in half with a sharp knife: Don't saw. Just press the knife down through the dough. Form each piece into a rectangle eight inches high and four inches across. Fold down the top two-thirds of the dough and press. Fold up the bottom two-thirds and press. Fold the top down all the way so that the top and bottom meet. Press the edges closed. Turn the loaf over so that the seam is on the counter and roll the dough back and forth gently five to eight times to smooth the seam. Place each loaf into a prepared pan, seam side down.

Cover the two pans with a dry cloth and leave the covered pans on the counter. Set a timer for fifteen minutes. When the timer rings, turn the oven on to 400° F. Again, set the timer for fifteen minutes. When the timer goes off again, it's time to prepare your oven.

It is important to add moisture to the oven; the moisture keeps the crust from forming too soon and allows the loaf to rise again. Moisture also aids in the caramelization of the crust. There are lots of ways to create steam in an oven. Some are better than others, but none is totally effective. After exploring many methods, I now choose to toss a tray of ice cubes into the hot oven just before I put the loaves in to bake. This method works well in gas ovens, but if you use an electric oven, you should be careful about letting the ice hit the heating coils. If you prefer not to use ice cubes, you can use a spray bottle to spray water along the oven walls. Wait two minutes and spray again. The ice cubes or sprayed water create dramatic steam. If you have young children in your household, they will love this part.

After the two fifteen-minute time periods, the loaves should have risen for the third time. Make sure that the dough doesn't rise over the top of the pan. If a loaf rises too much in the pan, it has no action left for the baking, when it should deflate a bit and rise the fourth time. If you see the dough reach the top of the pans, you'll need to cut the third rising short. If you don't catch it in time, don't worry; the bread will still be very good. It will simply look homemade!

Just before baking, use a very sharp knife to make a quarter-inch-deep slit down the middle of each loaf. Put both loaves on a rack positioned in the lower third of the oven and bake for forty minutes, until the top crust has a rich brown color.

Remove the finished loaves from their pans. The bread is done if it sounds hollow when tapped. You must let the loaves cool completely before slicing them; bread continues to cook as it cools. If you want to serve bread warm, cool it first and then put it back into a 400° F oven, directly on the oven rack, for ten to fifteen minutes.

Congratulations! You now know how to make a basic loaf of bread. When you try it again, experiment by adding a few tablespoons of chives and four tablespoons of Parmesan cheese. For another variation—especially nice for breakfast, add raisins, walnuts, and cinnamon. Or, for dinner rolls, add dill and cheddar cheese, and bake the dough in oiled muffin tins, filling each tin about three quarters of the way.

CHAPTER THREE

The Mystery of Leaven

Thursday is my bread-baking day, so every Wednesday night I begin my preparations. I go to my refrigerator to retrieve the container of *levain** that has rested there, undisturbed but not forgotten, since the previous week. Wednesday night is when I feed it, revive it, make it ready to be used again on the following day.

Levain is a universal component of the best artisanal European bread. It is also called sourdough starter or *chef** or *biga**, depending on the country, the recipe, and the ratio of water to flour. A home baker needs only one container of levain, which is used, fed, and stored each week. I will tell you how to make it and maintain it at the end of this chapter. All you will need is flour, water, and time.

My levain is aromatic and lively; it smells fertile and fermented. Bubbles work their way up from within it, creating activity and height. Bubbles climb over bubbles, until—if I have left it alone too long—it collapses on itself, becoming like pancake batter. If the levain collapses, I can still use it to moisten dough and add depth of flavor. But no longer can it serve as the sole source of leavening; I will need to add yeast. Of course, this produces a loaf that will be different from what I had originally planned. If I were able to delay my baking, I could feed the levain again, stir it every few hours, and wait for it to return to its full active life. But I bake only on Thursdays. So I must pay attention and be vigilant.

THE CYCLE OF CREATION

When we pay attention to the mysterious and hidden process of fermentation, we sense that it represents a small part of the universal cycle of creation. Life is being breathed into lifelessness. Form is emerging from formlessness. We take a paste of flour and water, add leavening, and create something that is new, living, and breathing. In a small way we become participants in the divine pattern established when God took mud, breathed life into it, and created Adam. (Gen. 2:7) Likewise, when we mold anything using the labor of our hands, we become co-creators with God.

The process of baking bread puts us intimately in touch with the cycle of creation: the life, death, and rebirth common to all organisms. The living, breathing, vital levain, which transforms dough from formless paste into a small feast, must die. It must be killed by the heat of the oven in order for there to be a new creation: a completed loaf of bread. Yet the same oven's heat also allows the loaf to rise a final time, and in so doing, it produces that which can feed a hungry world. Each time we bake a loaf of bread, we participate symbolically in God's promise, "See, I am making all things new." (Rev. 21:5)

LEAVEN'S LESSONS

Levain has taught me other lessons, reminding me of my limitations, showing me that I don't have ultimate control. My responsibility is to feed the levain, keep it warm, and replenish its food supply; but its action and power lie within itself, not with me. I might like to think that I have done something to make the leavening work. But all I have done is to participate in its nature. I can no more change its nature than I can change the nature of the kingdom of God.

Leavening was discovered, historians believe, when an ancient Egyptian baker, either lazy or careless, left a paste of flour and water in the sun all day, where it started to rot. Yeast cells caused the paste to bubble and swell. Instead of throwing it away, this baker took a handful of the fermented mass and added it to the next day's flour and water, creating an airier loaf than the usual flat bread. Bakers learned to replicate this result by holding back a portion of the fermented mixture for the next day's baking.

In the gospels of Matthew and Luke, Jesus compares the kingdom of God to yeast. (Mt. 13: 33; Lk 13:20-21) Our modern sensibilities might reject the comparison. How can this fungus be like the kingdom of God? I can offer several answers: leaven is transformative, working its mystery quietly as it enriches our lives. Leaven may be overlooked at first glance, but it can be identified if we are attentive to the signs of its presence. Leaven's inherent rottenness is exactly what is required to create life in the dough. But to become aware of these truths we need to pay attention.

ATTENTIVENESS

Attentiveness is a quality we should strive to develop. It is similar to alertness, but it has a broader focus and involves heightened perception. It is a different kind of seeing, particularly desirable for anyone who is searching for signs of the kingdom of God.

Attentiveness is not the frozen alertness of a child who sits in the classroom, waiting in terror for the teacher to ask the one question whose answer is utterly unknown. Yet such frozen alertness may even be an aid to achieving attentiveness. A doctor once told me of his medical school experience with an especially formidable professor. My friend and other students lived in dread of being the target of his arbitrary and fearsome questioning during grand rounds. Many years later, when my friend was an established and respected physician, he encountered his erstwhile professor, and they began to reminisce. It was then that the professor explained his teaching method: he knew full well that the student he singled out might be paralyzed by fear, unable to articulate an answer. But he knew also that the ability of all of the other students to remember would be heightened. He was forcing them to be attentive.

How—and where—are we to search for signs of the kingdom of God? On a beautiful spring day when the azaleas suddenly burst into bloom it is easy to see the signs and to be grateful to God. It is much more difficult to see God's hand at work when we are caught in the midst of life's trials. Are we able to believe that God also gives blessings by transforming rottenness and decay? Can we see signs of the eternal Easter that lies hidden in every Good Friday? Yes. But again we must pay attention, and paying attention is a risky business.

REFLECTIONS IN THE DARK PLACES

I find that it is risky to sit in my kitchen and be attentive to the work of the leavening. My thoughts travel through dark places on their way to the hope of Easter. There is pain on this journey because the leaven is rotten, and it is easy for me to forget that goodness will emerge from pain, suffering, and sorrow.

I invite you to risk attentiveness to your life. Begin by recalling your connectedness to all who share your life, especially those who frequently come through your kitchen. If you are honest with yourself, you realize that you cannot be everything that each of them wants you to be. Nor can your relationship with any one of them be everything you might hope for. Seeing the flaws in people and in relationships between and among people can even lead to questions about our having been created in the image of God. Maybe you have dreamed that certain of these relationships would be sufficient for you. But your dreams have turned to brittle memories that bring no joy today, and you sense a hollow pit where love should be. But don't stop your journey here.

Pay attention. The yeast is bubbling, filling the dough with holes. The hollowness you feel can seem like the absence of light and hope. But just as the holes in the dough are filled with gas, your hollow pit is filled with truth. Your truth is a mixture unique to your life, a recipe assembled from ingredients that range through disappointment, failure, shame, and fear. We may be terrified to lean over and look into this threateningly dark pit, fearing we will see some horrible reflection of ourselves.

Like the psalmist, we reach out for help:

> *But as for me, my prayer is to you, O LORD. At an acceptable time, O God, in the abundance of your steadfast love, answer me. With your faithful help, rescue me from sinking in the mire; let me be delivered from my enemies and from the deep waters. Do not let the flood sweep over me, or the deep swallow me up, or the Pit close its mouth over me.*
>
> (Ps. 69:14-17)

THROUGH DEATH TO LIFE

What is the worst terror this pit might reveal? Perhaps it is the dread of death—your own death. Perhaps what you see is not death as a gateway to the glories of eternity, but death as an on-ramp to eternal solitude, alienation, and darkness. You see the yeast of rottenness and decay, not the yeast of a new creation. Will there really be release from this terror with the coming of the kingdom of God? Be attentive.

17

Holy God, Holy and Mighty,
Holy and merciful Savior,
Deliver us not into the bitterness of eternal death.

(The Book of Common Prayer, p. 492, Burial Office)

Pay attention. Perhaps what you see reflected back is a lie that has entrapped you, grabbed your ankles, and thrown you to the ground. A lie will hobble the one who lives it. A lie is not just a choice; it is a lifestyle. It matters hardly whether the lie is of our own will or of someone else's; when we look into the dark reflection we will see only our face. Is this face welcome in the kingdom of God? We can identify with the apostle Paul, who wrote:

> *I do not understand my own actions. For I do not do what I want, but I do the very*
> *thing I hate.*

(Rom. 7:15)

It is difficult to remain attentive if the reflection brings us pain—a pain so private and intimate that it has been deeply buried, a pain whose existence we have successfully denied for years at a time. But now it is rising, stirred by an unwelcome memory. Perhaps this pain is the residue of times of betrayal and selfishness—all that remains when love has burned itself out. The rottenness of this pain is overwhelming. In our kitchen, the yeast smells sour. Can we still look on this rising dough with pleasure?

Often, shame is the source, the origin, of this pain. We are ashamed that we lost our temper when we promised ourselves that *this* time we wouldn't. We are ashamed that our gratitude was so paltry when the gift was so precious. We are ashamed that our first thoughts have been for our own comfort. Sadly, this pain does not go down to the grave with the death of the one we hurt or the one who hurt us. We are ashamed even to approach the gates of the kingdom of God.

These are bitter truths indeed, these "truths" of our lies, our pain and, our shame. How very rotten to the core they can make us believe we are. No one can be totally free from the leavening of guilt and shame. But the kingdom of God is made up of just such as these: a little fungus and decay—a little yeast. With this new view of the kingdom of God, we feel encouraged to take the next step.

But before we can taste the enriching, abundant new loaf of the kingdom, the yeast must complete its task and surrender to the heat of the oven. What we must first navigate is, very plainly, our fear of death: death from our lies, our pain, and our anxiety. When I run into people of my own age, middle age, whom I have not seen in a while, the conversation takes what is now a predictable path. We quickly dispense with news of the recent past and the present moment, and the conversation turns to such topics as retirement plans, 401(k)s, and long-term care insurance. If the conversation goes on long enough, the real topic emerges from all the facts and figures. Very simply, people our age die, and we are scared. How can we take to heart God's promise of resurrected life that awaits us just beyond this fearful cross of hope gone stale?

GLIMPSING NEW CREATION

In the quiet of your kitchen, you might want to name each of your fears, and substitute them for the words in this passage from Romans:

> For I am convinced that neither **death**, nor **life**, nor **angels**, nor **rulers**, nor **things present**, nor **things to come**, nor **powers**, nor **height**, nor **depth**, nor anything else in all creation, will be able to separate us from the love of God in Christ Jesus our Lord.
>
> (Rom. 8:38-39)

Be attentive. The bread is baking. Old memories are rising from Paul's litany of uncertainties. We remember moments of joy and keen awareness that God makes all things new: watching a cherished baby take her very first step, glimpsing a fledgling cardinal on its first visit to our feeder. When we pay attention, we may witness wonderful and glorious things.

Such moments of grace arrive unbidden. One came to me on a late autumn afternoon in Maine as I was driving from Blue Hill to Ellsworth. Ahead of me, I saw a sky with gray layer upon gray layer, endless gray on gray. Then suddenly without warning—no shifting in the gray—the late afternoon sunlight broke through the clouds. Just as quickly, and again with no warning, the sunlight was gone. But I was left with a new way of seeing the gray, a new way of seeing the clouds, the deep red leaves on each distinct tree, and the granite in its bed of russet blueberry bushes. Although I drove on, leaving that transfigured scene behind, it seemed to me that I carried with me the memory of a golden moment in the sun. It was as though an unseen divine hand had touched the bleak fall afternoon in northern New England.

We are promised that the kingdom of God is with us now. Right now. Its presence must surely feel like that moment of pure gold. When the grace of God breaks through our pain and through our shame, it is as though the late afternoon sun of autumn has blessed the gray landscape of our souls.

THE LIGHT OF GOD'S LOVE

When we are living in the dark pit of our anxieties—in our secret places—God seeks to come to us, to be in union with us. Paradoxically, when we are in darkness God's light can be more compelling; light is not visible in light. By God's grace we can allow the light of God's unconditional love to shine in our dark places, to overcome the fear of death, and to bring us hope. The yeast has died, and it has brought forth the first fruits of a newly created loaf.

In my book-study group, Kathy, one of the members once recounted an incident from her childhood. She described the moment when she first sensed that God's love was truly unconditional. Kathy told us she had been a very irresponsible and selfish little girl. She left toys around the house and yard. She didn't do her chores. She paid very little attention to the world around her. Kathy's most beloved doll was one victim of her inattention. This old-fashioned doll had a composition face which couldn't tolerate getting wet. One day Kathy left the doll out in the rain. When she found her doll all in a mess, she was heartbroken. She ran to her father and begged him to fix the doll's face. Her father held her in his arms and gently and lovingly told her that her doll's face was ruined beyond repair. Kathy remembers being shocked, as if there had been a death in the family.

As an adult, Kathy has come to understand that at that moment she glimpsed the nature of the kingdom of God. Her lesson that day certainly taught her to be more mindful of the things entrusted to her. But the deeper lesson was that her thoughtlessness and heartache had led her to the mystery of unconditional love. The kingdom of God requires us to pay attention to our actions, intentions and responsibilities. But when we don't, in spite of our failures, we will remain encircled in love. Yes, the yeast does leaven the loaf.

Baking a loaf of bread gives us time for meditation and prayer. When I smell my levain and watch it work its way through the flour, I have time to meditate on my dark places. And I look for the new creation that all who believe in God's promises will find. The kingdom of God is with us if we are attentive to its signs. So let's make the levain as a place to begin this discovery of love.

How to Make Levain
(Yield: Infinite!)

Flour

Water

You will need a container with a capacity of at least one gallon. A plastic one is fine, as long as its lid fits tightly and it is large enough for the levain to become very lively without blowing off the lid.

As I've mentioned, I recommend measuring ingredients by weight. Use a metric kitchen scale that has a tare feature that can subtract the weight of your container.

DAY ONE

50 grams (¼ cup) water

40 grams (⅓ cup) flour

Measure the water and flour. Mix them together, but do not worry about getting all the lumps out. Stir the mixture six to eight times throughout the day. The stirring is very important: it adds the oxygen that is needed for fermentation. *Do not refrigerate the levain at any time during the six-day process. Simply leave it on the counter, covered.*

DAY TWO

200 grams (¾ cup) water

160 grams (1½ cups) flour

Add the water and flour to the original flour-and-water mixture. Again, stir this mixture throughout the day.

DAY THREE

200 grams (¾ cup) water

160 grams (1½ cups) flour

Measure out 90 grams (⅓ cup) of the mixture and throw the rest down the drain. Rinse the container. Mix the water and flour. Add the reserved 90 grams of the original mixture. Stir.

DAY FOUR

200 grams (¾ cup) water

160 grams (1½ cups) flour

Repeat the previous day's process. By now, you should notice that the mixture is producing a rich and pungent aroma.

DAY FIVE

450 grams (2 cups) water

355 grams (3 cups) flour

Measure out 200 grams (¾ cup) of the mixture. Throw the rest down the drain. Rinse the container. Mix the water and flour. Add the reserved 200 grams of the mixture. Stir.

You now have levain that is ready to use. Each time you bake, your first step should be to reserve 200 grams (¾ cup) of your levain and feed it according to the instructions for Day Five. That reserved mixture will be your starter for your next batch of bread. You do not want to lose it! If your levain should collapse, feed it once in the morning and once in the evening, and by the next day, it should be just fine. Pay attention. Once I was carrying on a conversation while I was feeding my levain. Without thinking, I threw the whole thing down the drain and had to start from scratch. Back to Day One!

As time goes on, and the seasons change, you will notice that your levain changes, too. Depending on the room temperature and the moisture in your flour, your levain can be as smooth as pancake batter or as bubbly as scalding milk. If I have not plans to use my levain for several days, I cover it tightly and store it in the refrigerator. Then, the day before I bake, I follow the Day Five recipe: I measure out 200 grams, throw the rest away, rinse the container, and add 450 grams (2 cups) of water and 355 grams (3 cups) of flour. You shouldn't let your levain go for more than a week without a feeding. Don't worry if it separates; simply stir it well.

If you are going to be away from home for more than a week, find a trusted friend to feed your levain. It helps if the friend has a sense of humor! Recently, my husband and I were away for two months. Just before we left I took the levain, my metric scale, and flour to a friend's house. Our friend faithfully fed the levain once a week and kept it alive. But he told us that he couldn't wait to be rid of the responsibility once we returned. That's as it should be; to be involved with levain is to commit to the entire scope of the baking process. With this leaven we learn how to be co-creators within God's creation, discovering the blessings of divine love on our journey from sorrow to hope.

CHAPTER FOUR

I am passionate about baking bread. My love affair with baking began one summer when I was a teenager. My parents were on an extended trip, so my older brother and I, left on our own, decided to acquire some skills that would let us live as economically as possible. We thought we would save money if I baked all our bread. With no prior experience, I turned to James Beard's book *Beard on Bread* and followed all his directions for baking ordinary white bread. Though I doubt we saved even a nickel, that summer's discovery set me on the path of joy I still travel.

For years I made bread on my days off. Somehow, I knew that it was an important use of my "Sabbath" time. And I reveled in sharing the finished products with my family and friends, in donating it for sale at church fairs, or in giving it to friends and relatives in times of illness or sadness. Everything about this process touched my soul— the ingredients, each stage of preparation, and finally, the hot loaf of bread. But why? Why did this particular activity engage my spiritual self so deeply? Why could I catch more glimpses of God when I was baking than when I was kneeling in church? What was I being led to learn about the nature of God and about myself as a creature of God? These were the haunting questions that pursued me in my explorations as a baker. Where was I to go next? Back to school!

The French Culinary Institute (FCI) in New York City teaches the art of baking traditional artisanal European bread: everything from French baguettes to German seed breads, from Italian peasant loaves to Arabic pita. I enrolled to pursue my passion; I was on a spiritual

THE BREAD OF REMEMBRANCE

quest. My fellow classmates were restaurant owners and professional bakers looking to learn more about bread baking for their businesses. Upon completion of the course, we each were awarded a *Diplôme du Boulanger,** a Diploma of Baking.

I loved every minute I spent at the FCI. I loved the traditional uniforms, and I loved the long, hot labor. But mostly I loved mastering a craft that so completely centered me. I believed I had finally allowed myself to be led to the one activity that daily carried my soul to God.

At the French Culinary Institute, students learn why flour, water, salt and yeast do what they do to become bread. My weeks were filled with lessons about technique, chemistry, and traditional practices, as well as backbreaking labor, hot feet, and swollen ankles. Yet nothing I learned at the FCI answered my deepest questions: Why is bread so closely linked to my spiritual life? Why had bread become the icon, the window through which I caught glimpses of the divine?

My spiritual search kept moving me onward, driving me to the silence of my kitchen. There, through immersion in the unrefined and earthy ingredients of a loaf of bread, I opened myself to discoveries about God's grace in my life, about faith, about belief, and about unbelief.

MEMORIES OF FOOD AND COMPANIONSHIP

The bread I make—and the bread *we* are going to make—takes time. The process can take most of a day or in some instances, up to two days. We are not going to be making the bread of affliction, the unleavened bread the Israelites took with them when they fled Egypt in haste. (Ex. 12:39; Dt. 16:3) We have time to both harvest the yeast and to watch it leaven the entire dough. The action of yeast is slow, but it is as sure as the action of God's grace in our lives. We have time to sit and let memories wash over us. Let's see what comes to mind.

Over the last generation or two, as the pace of life in western culture has accelerated, we have given less and less priority to spending time with one another as fellow citizens, as fellow human souls. One dramatic example of this major shift has been the decline in family meal time. In studies conducted by the Harvard Medical School and Tufts University, researchers found in study of sixteen thousand children, among those aged nine years old, slightly more than half ate daily evening meals with members of their family, and by the time they were fourteen, that figure was only one third.[1] Jobs, sports practice, rehearsals, and lessons—our many obligations keep us from gathering the family around the dinner table. Our children are losing out: not only are they missing family companionship, they are also missing the experience of sharing family recipes, the typical foods of their household that might enrich in their adult years.

Why are food memories important? What do they evoke in us when we recall them throughout the decades of our lives? Food memories make us conscious of time in different ways. A long-forgotten aroma or taste can return us to the past while we remain in the present. Food memories can put us in touch with the mysterious.

For Marcel Proust the taste of a madeleine was the key to his memory. If you have ever eaten a madeleine, you might wonder that anyone would find it special. Yet for Proust, the taste was potent enough to inspire seven volumes of *The Remembrance of Things Past*. When I was a child, the special family treat was Junket. Our family dinners were not always pleasant experiences. No matter how distasteful the main dish was or how stern the parental rebuke, as children, we had to clean our plates. But then out would come Junket for dessert! Mom would let us have two or three servings if we wanted.

1. Quoted by Sheila Gains in "Family Mealtime: A Menu for Opportunities," found on the Colorado State University web site, www.ext.colostate.edu.

I remember the glass dishes and the sound of the spoon against the glass. I remember how the Junket tasted with lots of cinnamon on it. But mostly, I remember how loved it made me feel. A few years ago, I found some Junket in a grocery store and decided to have my own "madeleine moment". Unlike Proust, however, I found no bliss; in fact, I was surprised to find—as an adult—it tastes rather awful! Yet without those memories, my soul would have fewer experiences of love to sustain me.

My friend Andrea encountered her "madeleine moment" as she was preparing a batch of levain for the first time. The smell of the levain—the distinctive, pungent aroma of fermented flour and water—took her back to her childhood and to the restaurant and bakery her family owned in northern New Jersey. The smell captured memories of her father and grandfather and the odor of their arms and clothes. She remembered the bakery's oven, a huge wood-fired brick oven about three feet high and twenty feet deep. Andrea's task at the age of five or six was to climb into the cold oven with a dust pan and broom and to sweep out the burnt cornmeal from the previous day's baking. Afterward, she would watch her father prepare the dough for pizza and Italian bread. Those forgotten moments returned to her in a rush with the smell of the levain. The aroma of the first bread Andrea baked with levain connected her past and her present family in a mysterious way, merging and enlarging her memories of companionship and love.

CHURCH SUPPERS

I once heard about a church-planning consultant who was hired by a congregation in an upper-middle class suburb in northern California. The congregation was looking for ways to make the daily experience of the Gospel more real to their members. The consultant shrewdly suggested that they gather more often for church suppers and fellowship. But, being aware of the congregation's busy lifestyle, he suggested that these suppers be catered.

I can't tell you how strongly I disagree with his suggestion! In serving a catered meal, the community loses an opportunity to prepare food together and to share family recipes. Food traditions, even quirky ones, become a vital part of a church's life. "You're going to bring your kielbasa casserole again, right?" Or "You know she'll bring that Jell-O salad again, even though it's right out of the fifties!" If our church supper is catered we miss having wonderful stories about when we first ate a particular dish, who taught us to make it, and what it reminds us of. We lose a little of the texture of who we are. We miss out on sharing a corner of our souls with someone else.

EMERGING INSIGHTS

Come with me now, and we'll bake. And let us be open to new insights while we work. Once we have mixed the dough, it will need our attention for only a few brief periods. The rest of the day, we can go about our business and live our lives. And the dough will wait for us to come back to it. This characteristic of bread dough might be the first spiritual insight bread has for us. As the dough waits for our return, so God always waits patiently for us. We don't have to have strayed as far as the prodigal son. (Lk. 15:11-32) Whenever and from wherever we come back to God, our return is an occasion for a celebration. Baking also helps us take time to wait on God as God waits on us.

Usually, when I bake in my kitchen at home, I am alone. I am no stranger to aching loneliness, and I doubt that you are, either. Few of us have escaped its crushing pain. At some point in life's journey we become aware of God's offer to fill our loneliness, but we hesitate to abandon our self-will, our pride, and anything else that keeps us from admitting that we need God. In the silence of my kitchen I knead the dough and observe the living yeast working from within to leaven my bread. Gradually, I realize that I am not alone. I am in the presence of life—this leaven—and also in the presence of God: if only I have eyes to see. I breathe deeply and catch a hint—a whiff—of that life. I catch the aroma of God.

Even before we take our loaves from the oven, their aroma permeates the air. A home filled with the scent of freshly baked bread signifies a warm and cozy haven. Every week a friend comes for tea. She holds a difficult corporate job at which she succeeds with grace and integrity. But its demands take their toll. In our conversations over countless pots of tea, we have dwelt on our childhoods, our adult dreams, and tomorrow's surprises. As the intimacy of our conversations grew, I gradually realized that I could minister to my friend and her soul's wounds by surrounding her with the warmth and aroma of baking. So I changed my normal baking day to the day she comes to visit. From the moment she walks through the door to the moment she leaves she senses that she is "home," safe, loved, and accepted. To bake a loaf of bread as an act of hospitality while listening to someone whose spirit is troubled, is to demonstrate God's unconditional hospitality toward us all.

Our loaves are finished. One cooled loaf is lying in pieces on the cutting board after our taste test. The other two are ready to be wrapped and delivered to friends. To whom will you give yours? Why? Do you want your friends to feel indebted to you? I suggest that you give the loaves as a free gift, without expecting to receive anything in return. Imitate the unmerited gift of God's grace. I know that I rarely hear later whether or how my friends enjoyed the bread I gave them. Was it toast at breakfast? Slathered with butter and honey for an afternoon snack? Dipped in a hearty dinnertime stew? It doesn't really matter. People for whom I regularly bake have come to take my bread for granted, and I don't mind. When the giving is all on the baker's side, we practice the free offering of ourselves; the bread becomes its tangible expression.

For God so loved the world that he gave his only Son, that whoever believes in him should not perish but have eternal life.

(Jn. 3:16)

LOVE THAT ABIDES

When I give away a loaf of homemade bread, I intend my action to be an exercise in unconditional love. Most of our love is conditional; on holidays, for instance, many people give presents to get them in return. Rarely do we witness truly selfless love—giving without hope of some kind of return. Quite by chance, though, I was privileged to witness one incident that sticks in my mind.

Several years ago in Bar Harbor, Maine, my husband and I went out to dinner to celebrate our wedding anniversary. We were anticipating a romantic, expensive evening of self-indulgent pleasure. The restaurant we chose had once been a private house, and each of its small rooms could hold no more than six or eight tables. The room in which we were seated filled rapidly until only one table remained unclaimed, the table nearest to us. The last couple arrived, and it was impossible not to notice them. They were poorly dressed; they apparently did not speak English; and the wife was in a wheelchair. With some difficulty, her husband maneuvered her chair directly across from me, seated himself behind me. There was barely room for him to move his chair without bumping into mine.

We soon realized that, although they appeared to be only in their thirties, the wife was completely disabled. She could not even speak. But her husband spoke to her lovingly in German. After settling himself, he got up and put her napkin in her lap. Then he sat down and took her picture. When their food came, he took a picture of it and described it to her in detail. Then again he took her picture. Next he got up and took some of the lobster from its shell and fed her. Again he took her picture. He was devotedly attentive to her every need. Soon, we noticed that the room had become completely quiet as each one of us was gathered into their romance.

Those two gave us the most precious anniversary present we have ever received: a vision of unconditional love. So far as we could see, the husband would receive nothing in return for loving his wife; nothing in return for bringing her from Germany to vacation in Bar Harbor; nothing in return for lavishing attention and thoughtful care on her. It appeared that his selfless love would endure until her death. He would continue to give all and receive nothing tangible in return.

In this life, most of us can catch only glimpses of such an abiding love. We search them out as examples of the unconditional love God has shown to humanity. And when we are able, we imitate them as best we can. Giving a loaf of bread is the way I know to put myself regularly in the path of this divine love. Come now; carry a loaf of love to someone in your world.

THE BREAD OF HOSPITALITY

Every loaf of bread offers the promise of welcome and hospitality. The promise is contained in the living process of fermentation that works on the mixture of flour, water, and salt. When Abraham and Sarah were surprised by a visit from three strangers, messengers of God, Sarah baked bread quickly in order to offer them hospitality. (Gen. 18) We bakers welcome the hope of a new creation each time we bake a new loaf.

This bread calls for three types of wheat to represent the three strangers to Abraham's tent. As they were heralds of a new promise, a covenant, between Abraham's descendants and God, let this bread be something new for you.

Sarah's Three-Wheat Bread
(Yield: three loaves)

465 grams (2 cups) levain

690 grams (5 cups) white flour

230 grams (1¾ cups) whole wheat flour

285 to 450 grams (1⅛ to 2 cups) water

1 teaspoon yeast

1 tablespoon salt

170 grams (1 cup) wheat berries, boiled for 20 minutes and soaked overnight at
  room temperature

When you measure the levain, be sure to reserve 200 grams (¾ cup) and feed it according to the instructions for Day Five. (See page 23.)

Combine all the ingredients except the wheat berries in a mixing bowl or in the bowl of a heavy-duty mixer fitted with the dough hook. Running your mixer at the lowest speed, mix for approximately two minutes. Alternatively, use a wooden spoon to mix manually until all the ingredients have become incorporated. Either way, drain the wheat berries and add them to your dough. On Speed 2, mix for another four to five minutes, or until the dough is shiny and satiny. Or working manually, knead the dough on a well-floured surface for six to ten minutes, adding flour as needed until the dough is soft but still shiny and damp. Return the dough to the mixing bowl. For the first rising, place the bowl in a steam-filled microwave or cover it with a warm damp cloth and put it in a draft-free place. (See Hint 4, page 93.) The dough will not rise much during the first rising.

After the dough has been rising for one hour, place it directly on a well-floured surface. Degas the dough: Sprinkle flour on top of the dough and press down gently, releasing air. Fold the dough in half, bringing the top to the bottom. Press lightly and fold the dough in half from side to side twice, pressing after each fold. Sprinkle a little flour in the bowl and return the dough to the bowl. Put it back in its rising place for the second rising, another hour.

Dust three willow baskets* liberally with flour or oil three nine-by-five-inch loaf pans. Pour the dough onto a well-floured surface and cut it into three equal pieces.

If you are using willow baskets, flour your hands and form the three pieces into separate balls: Pull the top over the middle and seal with your fingertips. Turn the dough one-quarter turn and repeat. Do this again. Now turn the dough so that the seam side is down. Cup your hands around the sides of the ball and a little under it. Roll the ball around a bit to seal the seam and to smooth the top. (This takes some practice.) Place each ball into a basket, seam side up. If you are going to be baking your loaves on a baking stone, put the stone on a rack in the lower third of the oven.

If you are baking in loaf pans, flour your hands and form the three pieces into logs just smaller than your pans: Form each piece into a rectangle about five inches wide and seven inches long. Fold the top down to just below the halfway point and seal it with your fingertips. Fold the bottom up to just above the halfway point and seal. Fold the top down so that it is even with the bottom and seal. With your hands cupped around the length of the log and slightly under it, rock the log back and forth to seal the seam and to smooth out the top slightly. Place each log in its pan with the seam side down.

Cover the dough-filled baskets or pans with a cloth and set them on your counter for the third rising. After twenty minutes, preheat the oven to 460° F and wait twenty minutes more. When the oven has reached baking temperature, add moisture by tossing in a tray of ice cubes or spraying water from a spray bottle. (See Hint 6, page 94.)

If you have used willow baskets, flour the baker's peel and tip one loaf from its basket onto the peel. (See Hint 7, page 94.) The dough might stick to the basket. If it does, gently pull it off and reform the ball on the peel by tucking the sides under. Score the top of the loaf by cutting a quarter-inch-deep cross with a sharp knife, razor blade, or *lame**. Slide the loaf onto the preheated baking stone in the oven. Bake for fifty minutes. The remaining two loaves can stay in their baskets on the counter if your kitchen is cool. If the kitchen is quite warm, cover the third basket tightly with plastic wrap and place it in the refrigerator, returning it to the counter when you put the second loaf into the oven. Remember to score each loaf and to add a tray of ice cubes to the oven just before baking.

If you are baking in loaf pans, score each loaf with one lengthwise cut, one-quarter-inch deep, and bake all three loaves at once. Bake for fifty minutes on a rack placed in the lower third of the oven.

This bread is done when it is a deep golden brown, the top is hard, and it sounds hollow when you tap it. Cool completely before slicing.

And last, but not least: if you plan to give away any of the loaves, be sure to tell your family so that nobody will eat your gift before you can deliver it!

CHAPTER FIVE

D aily life is, frankly, ordinary. Learning to live in the grace of ordinary life is one of the most difficult challenges we encounter as we grow and mature.

In our youth, we imagine that a life lived from thrill to thrill, or from peak to peak, would be exciting and fulfilling. In fact, such a pattern of life is exhausting and potentially dangerous. But in our exuberance, we are afraid that if we were to stop seeking thrills, our lives would feel hollow; we would have to settle for what is bland, unremarkable, and boring. We fear that unless we live life deeply, we may miss something. How terrible it would be if someone else overtook us in the race; what a blow to our competitive selves if we didn't push to win all the prizes!

We also might have to settle for less than instant gratification. We are never far removed from the days of foot-stomping tantrums and whining, "I want it, and I want it *now*!"

Thrill-seeking and competitiveness effectively shield us from seeing ourselves with honest eyes. When we choose to be free of distracting influences, we will have to face ourselves, our less-dramatic inner landscape, and the truth that we are neither so deep nor so special as we think we are. Discarding this illusion is the hardest task of all. What remains, in short, is that we are ordinary.

LIVING ORDINARY LIVES

ORDINARY BREAD

There are few tasks more ordinary than baking a loaf of bread. I remember watching a baker in a small Portuguese village as she prepared the dough for the morning's bread. Zefa began her day as she had begun countless other days. Quiet, professional, with no wasted movements or sense of rush, her work manifested her implicit belief in the inherent dignity of her work. She mixed the water and flour using an enormous ceramic platter as a bowl. She measured nothing, not even the salt or the yeast.

I stood near Zefa and watched in the cool silence of the spring morning. The only sound came from the wood oven as the kindling burned. Zefa made no clumsy or unnecessary movements. Never looking up, she simply kneaded the dough with her knuckles. I was awed by the strength of her hands and arms. The muscles in her upper arms strained against the uniform she wore. Eventually, she stopped kneading, knowing by its feel that the dough was ready.

Without acknowledging that I was watching so closely, Zefa gently divided the dough into quadrants with her forefinger and made a single depression in each quadrant. I was immediately curious and gestured for her to explain. What is that? Why you did do that? She shrugged her shoulders, looking at me with a hint of a smile that expressed her wonder and amusement at my ignorance.

As I am unable to speak Portuguese, I asked someone who spoke enough English to interpret. She explained that "when Zefa draws the line going from top to bottom she says, 'God raises you up.' With the line across she says, 'The angels look over you.' Then, starting at the top right corner and going clockwise she says, 'In the name of the Father · and of the Son · and of the Holy Spirit. · Amen.'"

I looked again at the platter of dough already beginning to rise in the warm kitchen. Only a hint of Zefa's marks remained. After the loaf had been baked her marks would no longer be visible, and the world would see only an ordinary loaf of plain white bread. But I knew better. In essence, this ordinary loaf had become Zefa's prayer for all of us.

FILLING THE EMPTY PLACES

Why is it so hard for us to appreciate the things we label "ordinary"? Why do we crave what is "35 percent more," "bigger than ever," and "under new management"? I believe that the key is found in the distraction that "newness" can bring to our lives. Without distraction, our cares soon overwhelm us.

Turning to the psalms, we find that we are not alone in this very human yearning for relief from emptiness and sorrow:

> *Be gracious to me O LORD, for I am in distress, and my eyes are dimmed with grief. My life is worn away with sorrow and my years with sighing.*
>
> (Ps. 31:9-10)

> *I am wearied with groaning; all night long my pillow is wet with tears, I soak my bed with weeping. Grief dims my eyes; they are worn out with all my woes.*
>
> (Ps. 6:6-7)

We yearn to be touched to our depths, to have our empty places filled. We ache to be seen, known, and treasured. We are a like a people bereaved, and there is no peace in us.

Bereavement can envelop us like a cold shadow whether or not we are mourning an actual death. I have known people who have no apparent cause for bereavement, yet they are consumed with grief over the death of hope in their lives. I have met other people whose situations and experiences leave me wondering how they can get out of bed each day, yet they persevere because they never lose hope.

There is no sadness greater than the sadness of hopelessness. It can be a huge crushing weight on your chest, asphyxiating you and leaving you with seemingly inescapable fear and nausea. Lying awake at 3:00 a.m., sweating and gasping for air, some of us have even grasped in our hands the means for ending our despair. There are as many reasons for hopelessness as bedside lights burning long after the neighborhood has settled down for sleep. If only all the wakeful, quaking souls could know they are not alone—that they are bound together by their struggles and by their loss. Together, they could take the first step from bereavement to hope.

The ancient psalmist sang of the hope that is freely available to everyone who calls upon God for help:

> *Depend upon the LORD, and he will grant you your heart's desire. Commit your life to the LORD; trust in him and he will act.*
>
> (Ps. 37:4-5)

> *You who live in the shelter of the Most High, who abide in the shadow of the Almighty, will say to the Lord, 'My refuge and my fortress; my God, in whom I trust.' For he will deliver you from the snare of the hunter and from the deadly pestilence. . . . You will not fear the terror of the night, or the arrow that flies by day, the pestilence that stalks in darkness, or the destruction that wastes at noonday.*
>
> (Ps. 91:1-3,5-6)

My parish has found an effective weapon with which we fight against hopelessness among the homeless. We host a program whose mission is not just finding housing but also resurrecting lives and restoring hope. David and Donna were two young people who participated in that program. They spent their nights sleeping in church classrooms and their days being trained for new jobs. Each of them found new strength and new hope in their lives, and that hope caused them to ask to be married in church. Nothing holds more hope and promise than a wedding, so on a March afternoon, I sat in a pew and wept along with family members and other program volunteers as we witnessed the consecration of their hope. David and Donna were not defeated by the "pestilence" of homelessness. And we celebrated their newfound hope with great joy.

BREAD AS AN ICON OF HOPE

How may we be agents of hope for others? We might offer a tender word, a gentle touch, a gift of our time, or perhaps a gift of plain white bread as a symbol or icon of hope.

Michael Nissenblatt, an oncologist in central New Jersey, has treated hundreds of patients for whom hope is elusive. He has sat with them and listened to their despair, to how they are even afraid of their fear. He has waited with them as they struggled to find meaning in the chaos of their diseases. He has held their hands as they faced their shock at losing the sense of themselves as whole, healthy human beings.

Dr. Nissenblatt brings to each patient not just his medical skill and art, but also his spirit nurtured by the traditions of Judaism. One important symbol in Judaism is the challah, a braided white bread that Jews bless and eat in their homes each Friday night. It serves as a weekly reminder of new life and resilience—a symbol of hope.

One Friday in 1993, Dr. Nissenblatt bought a loaf of challah on his way to the hospital where he was planning to check on his patients. One of his patients, an elderly woman with multiple myeloma, was suffering considerable pain. He saw that this woman, who was an observant Jew, was losing hope, fearing that all she had to look forward to was more pain and more suffering. Her despair triggered a response in Dr. Nissenblatt—a response from the very core of his being. He excused himself and went to the hospital's parking garage where he retrieved the challah. Returning to his patient's room, he gave her the challah, and she accepted it from his hands as a symbol of life and hope. Right then, he could see that despair was leaving her; the gift of the bread had restored her hope.

Soon after that encounter, Dr. Nissenblatt began to buy extra challahs on Fridays, and he gave them to his Jewish patients. One day, the non-Jewish roommate of one of his patients asked him why he gave loaves of bread only to certain people. That question prompted him to give a challah every Friday to all his patients regardless of their religion. Every one of his patients craved the hope and life the bread symbolizes. The challah had become another of Dr. Nissenblatt's tools for healing, for reviving his patients' spirits and renewing their outlook on life.

Before long Dr. Nissenblatt was distributing as many as fifty loaves each Friday, and he could no longer handle pick-up and delivery on his own. Two men who had lost their wives to cancer volunteered to pick up loaves at a local bakery and distribute them on his behalf. Since 1993, about 20,000 challahs have been given away, each one representing an immeasurable quantity of hope.

I know Dr. Nissenblatt's story because I am a frequent visitor to the gravely ill patients in his same cancer unit, 2-Core at the Robert Wood Johnson University Hospital. Whenever I pass by the nurses' station, I look up at a photograph hanging there: it captures one of thousands of moments of love and hope. The patient in the photograph, a

Colombian woman with breast cancer, was undergoing a difficult preparation for a bone marrow transplant. She spoke no English. At first, she could not comprehend why the doctor was offering her a loaf of bread. There was a struggle to communicate. Finally understanding dawned, and the photograph captures a luminous spirit of promise as she reaches up to receive her challah from Dr. Nissenblatt's hands. For me, this powerful picture has become a constant reminder of the beauty of hope that is offered through the ordinary stuff of life.

CHOOSING AN ORDINARY LIFE

When people refer to the everyday pejoratively as "just plain white bread," they are implying that no sophisticated person would choose what is ordinary. For women, an additional implication has been that staying at home with a family is too ordinary, and that only women who work outside the home are valued, fulfilled, or complete.

But more and more, women are telling me that they are trying to back away from careers that have them trapped in patterns of aggressive sophistication and exhausting performances. They have come to see the value of a life that is deeply rooted in the activities and ordinary tasks that sustain home life. These women do not repudiate the goals and gains of the women's movement. Rather, they understand that because of the achievements of the women's movement, women have earned a new freedom to return home.

Many women do not have the luxury of choosing to stay home; their income is essential to their families. I know that my family's decision to have me stay at home meant making a financial sacrifices. After a few dry runs at living on one salary, I "came home for good." But we had to revisit that decision, and eventually I returned to part-time work. Financial considerations aside, if you buck the pressure to pursue success, you open yourself to considerable criticism and even contempt. You need determination to live with this vulnerability, to live with the fear that the world may be passing you by. But if you choose this path, you will gain time to evaluate your life's decisions, to dream, and to discover unexpected gifts that are waiting for you.

If leaving the fast track is impossible, you can still search for brief interludes of respite. Whether you are able to stay home one day per week or you condense a whole year's worth of solitary time into a vacation, a retreat, or a snowy Saturday morning—no matter what the circumstances—there are always moments of peace to be discovered and cultivated. Hug them to yourself, embrace them, and return to them often. Grab hold of them and carry them with you when you head back into the fray.

I didn't realize just how fast I had been living until I slowed down. Once I was able to live the slower pace of daily life at home, I found time to grieve for bad decisions, for the haste that had caused me to miss the precious details that give texture to daily life. Conversations with my colleagues and friends still focused on the world I had left behind—a world in which I thought of myself as important and needed. Now it was their world and no longer mine. I had set out on a risky journey, and I had had to leave certain concerns behind me.

But the new world I had chosen to inhabit offered me more than enough to replace what I had lost. I rediscovered my voice that spoke to God and my ears that listened. Doing morning exercises, sharing coffee with friends, or running errands for the family, I felt God's touch as though for the first time. As I grew towards a new love for ordinary things, simple rituals became new dwelling places for God. Most especially, the time I set aside every week for the ritual of baking a loaf of bread became a time for me to focus on my risky journey home; and with the dough under my fingernails and on my arms, I caught a glimpse of peace. I learned to perceive the smell of freshly baked bread as a divine aroma, and just as Dr. Nisenblatt's patients filled themselves with the challah of hope, I filled myself with God's promises.

FOCUSING ON GOD

Do you know the story of the prophet Elijah? (1 Kings 19) Elijah was in crisis. Having obeyed God's voice, Elijah had taken terrible risks, and many angry people were looking for him. They wanted to kill him. He fled for his life and hid in a mountain cave. He was desperate to hear God's voice, to know what direction his life should take. As he stood on the mountain, a great wind arose, strong enough to break rocks. But God was not in the wind. An earthquake shook the mountain. But God was not in the earthquake. Fire swept the mountain. But God was not in the fire. "And after the fire, a sound of sheer silence." It was in this silence that God was to be found.

We, too, seek times of quiet in which we can know God's presence in our lives. In peace and quiet, we can find the courage to follow the pilgrim's path to closer union with God. For us, the "wind, earthquake and fire" that obscure God's voice may take the form of external busyness—the noise of the world. We can turn our backs on busyness, but even in solitude, our thoughts can be as loud and rambunctious as a millennial New Year's Eve party. For centuries people have used such aids to prayer as knotted ropes or rosaries, accompanied by repetitive prayers, to help focus the mind and open the heart to God. In a similar way, focusing on a simple, ordinary task can help in quiet our internal noise and become more receptive to the divine presence.

For more than a decade, I have helped other people articulate their questions about God and search for answers to those questions. My aim has been to help people grow in faith and wisdom, to help them see the hand of God in their lives. But recently a friend asked me directly about my own experience: had my understanding of God grown in the time since I chose the ordinariness of home life? What insights had come to me?

At first, I found her question slightly embarrassing. I admitted that I still carry some unsophisticated images of God—images I never left behind as I grew in age and in knowledge. We laughed together as she admitted to this, too. Still, I gave her question the thoughtful consideration it deserved. I told her that often when my hands are plunged into a sack of flour or are busy in the sink washing up my baking mess, my mind is quieted. In moments such as these, I have come to trust that God is present: wherever I am, God is there, too. God is as close as my next breath, filling the air I breathe.

God has been with me, is with me, and will be with me, even through panic-filled nights and lonely days, "even though I walk through the valley of the shadow of death." I now trust that God walks with me when I am lost in darkness and fear, when loneliness threatens to overwhelm me, and when I shed my tears of remorse. Even now, God is teaching me about divine love. When darkness envelops me, my task is to wait it out with trust and patience.

As I knead my dough and shape my loaves, my mind returns to the glimpses of God that have been revealed to me in the light and warmth of my kitchen. When two-year-old Isabel stretched out her tiny arms, wanting me to pick her up so she could laugh with me face to face, her trust and delight, her rowdy hilarity, showed me the face of God's humor. When our grown children began to ask for adult advice, amazed at how much smarter we are now than when they were teenagers, I sensed a new hint of God's acceptance. When I thought about all the inside jokes lovers share—jokes that never will be told again when one of them dies—I began to know how intimately God lives with us. When I became overwhelmed by all the second chances I had been given, I started to comprehend God's forgiveness. In the quiet and homeliness of my bread-baking kitchen, I give thanks for all these blessings.

CELEBRATING SIMPLICITY TOGETHER

Choosing to simplify our lives is risky and counter cultural. We need the support of other people who have made the same choice. We need companions on our journey, fellow seekers with whom we worship God and hear the promises again and again: God loves us, treasures us, cherishes us even when we are sitting in darkness. With these other seekers, we struggle to take the intellectual knowledge of God's promises into the depths of our souls where it can nourish us. At the same time we need to support each other as we reject the cultural values that urge us to satisfy the yearning in our souls by buying the latest high-tech gadget or watching one more mindless sitcom.

I know a place where people gather to celebrate the simple life. Every September thousands of people come to the tiny village of Unity, Maine, for one weekend. Unity's annual fair has all the elements common to other country fairs—with a difference. Although there are plenty of activities for children, this fair doesn't offer the mechanical rides on which the children would be passive. Instead, it has set aside a play area with fields of tall grass in which the children run and hide, and bales of hay they are invited to rip apart and mess up. The laughter from the play area is no less lively than the laughter from Coney Island's Cyclone. And like other country fairs, an enormous selection of food and beverage is available, but again, with a difference: everything is entirely organic, with no refined sugar or caffeine. After a day at this fair, everyone feels peace, not giddy enervation.

I invite you to consider your daily routine carefully. Move away from choices that drain you of your vitality. Seek the ordinary tasks that will lead you toward grace. As for me, I am going to bake bread for my friends. Whether or not you make the same choice, I pray that you will find what I have found: prayer and God's loving presence.

Just Plain White Bread
(Yield: three loaves)

1,000 grams (7½ cups) white flour

725 grams (2¾ cups) levain

450 grams (2 cups)water

3 teaspoons salt

1 teaspoon active dry yeast

When you measure the levain, be sure to reserve 200 grams (¾ cup) and feed it according to the instructions for Day Five. (See page 23.)

This dough can be difficult to work with because it is so sloppy. So don't try to knead it by hand. Use a mixer. The finished product is superb and worth the trouble.

Combine all the ingredients in the bowl of a heavy-duty mixer fitted with the dough hook. Running your mixer at the lowest speed, mix for approximately two minutes, until all the ingredients are incorporated. On Speed 2, mix for another four to five minutes, or until the dough is smooth and satiny. For the first rising, place the bowl in a steam-filled microwave or cover it with a warm damp cloth and put it in a draft-free place. (See Hint 4, page 93.) The dough will not rise much during the first rising.

After the dough has been rising for one hour, place it directly on a well-floured surface. Degas the dough: sprinkle flour on top of the dough and press down gently, releasing air. Fold the dough in half, bringing the top to the bottom. Press lightly and fold the dough in half from side to side twice, pressing after each fold. Sprinkle a little flour in the bowl and return the dough to the bowl. Put it back in its rising place for the second rising, another hour.

Dust three willow baskets liberally with flour or oil three nine-by-five-inch loaf pans. Pour the dough onto a well-floured surface and cut it into three equal pieces. It is hard to shape this dough. With well-floured hands form the three pieces into separate balls. To do this, pull the top over the middle and seal with your fingertips. Turn the dough one-quarter turn and repeat. Do this again. Now turn the dough so that the seam side is down. Cup your hands around the sides of the ball and a little under it. Roll the ball around a bit to seal the seam and to smooth the top. (This takes some practice.) Make them as round as you can. Then place them seam side down in the baskets. If you are going to be baking your loaves on a baking stone, put the stone on a rack in the lower third of the oven.

If you are baking in loaf pans, flour your hands and form the three pieces into logs just smaller than your pans: form each piece into a rectangle about five inches wide and seven inches long. Fold the top down to just below the halfway point and seal it with your fingertips. Fold the bottom up to just above the halfway point and seal. Fold the top down so that it is even with the bottom and seal. With your hands cupped around the length of the log and slightly under it, rock the log back and forth to seal the seam and to smooth out the top slightly. Place each log in its pan seam side down.

Cover the dough-filled baskets or pans with a cloth and set them on your counter for the third rising. After twenty minutes, preheat the oven to 460° F and wait twenty minutes more. When the oven has reached baking temperature, add moisture by tossing in a tray of ice cubes or spraying water from a spray bottle. (See Hint 6, page 94)

If you have used willow baskets, flour the baker's peel and tip one loaf from its basket onto the peel (see Hint 4, page 93.) The dough might stick to the basket. If it does, gently pull it off and reform the ball on the peel by tucking the sides under. Score the top of the loaf by cutting a quarter-inch-deep slash with a sharp knife, razor blade, or lame. Slide the loaf onto the preheated baking stone set in the oven. Bake for forty-five minutes. The remaining two loaves can stay in their baskets on the counter if your kitchen is cool. If the kitchen is quite warm, cover the third basket tightly with plastic wrap and place it in the refrigerator, returning it to the counter when you put the second loaf into the oven. Remember to score each loaf and to add a tray of ice cubes to the oven just before baking.

If you are baking in loaf pans, score each loaf with one lengthwise cut, one-quarter-inch deep, and bake all three loaves at once. Bake for forty-five minutes on a rack placed in the lower third of the oven.

This bread is done when it is a golden brown, the top is hard, and it sounds hollow when you tap it. Cool completely before slicing. Don't trouble yourself with how this bread looks. It tastes too good to matter.

For me, there is nothing more delicious than bread dipped in wonderful juices. I learned these two recipes at a cooking school in Portel, Alentejo, Portugal. Try serving them with your Just Plain White Bread. This combination makes a warm and comforting winter's supper.

Portuguese Black-Eyed Peas
(Yield: four-six servings)

1 pound black-eyed peas, soaked overnight, simmered until *al dente*, and drained

1 3-ounce can Italian tuna

3 tablespoons scallions, green part only, chopped

1 clove garlic, finely chopped

4 tablespoons cilantro, chopped

¼ cup extra-virgin olive oil

3 tablespoons white wine vinegar

Salt

Mix all the ingredients together. Refrigerate for a few hours.

Cilantro (Coriander) Soup
(Yield: four-six servings)

2 leeks, white part only, coarsely chopped

4 potatoes, peeled and coarsely chopped

7 tablespoons cilantro, chopped

4 tablespoons fresh dill, chopped

3 cloves garlic, finely chopped

¼ cup extra virgin olive oil

1 bunch kale, stems removed

Salt

Sour cream

Chop the kale and set it aside. Place leeks, potatoes, four tablespoons of the cilantro, dill, garlic, and olive oil in a large pot. Add water to cover by two inches. Bring the pot to a boil and simmer the vegetables until the potatoes are very soft, approximately fifteen minutes. Drain the vegetables, reserving the broth. Separately, boil the kale in water to cover until it is tender, approximately fifteen minutes. Drain the kale and add it to the other cooked vegetables. Puree the vegetables in a blender or food processor. Return the pureed vegetables to the reserved broth, reheat, add salt to taste, and mix in the remaining cilantro. Serve hot with sour cream.

CHAPTER SIX

Over the last fifteen years, I have stood at the altar in several parishes, where I served as an Episcopal priest and have offered consecrated bread to the congregation. At the little New Jersey Bayshore parish where I currently serve part-time, I stand again, humbled by the faces of the people who come week after week, year after year, to take and eat.

They come at all times of their lives. Some come as infants, innocent, still with laughing hearts and eager hands. Others are in their prime, heads held high. Still others are stooped by advancing years. Some people come with fear and hope and wonder. Some come with guilt or sorrow. They all come to be emptied of their need, to be filled by God instead.

> *This is the bread that came down from heaven, not like that which your ancestors ate, and they died. But the one who eats this bread will live forever.*
> (Jn. 6:58)

The consecrated bread serves as a powerful symbol of God's love and presence. Yet the bread is baked by human hands, from the basic materials of wheat, leavening, and water. It is brought to this particular church on this day to be offered back to God. Each loaf is a product of the relationship of its ingredients, human labor, and God's love. Knowing that all of life's provisions ultimately come as free gifts from God, we say, "All

TAKE AND EAT

things come of thee, O LORD, and of thine own have we given thee." Though this physical loaf may be consumed, the loaf of love can never be used up. The next time we gather for this holy meal, the bread will be here again, confirming that we never cease to be members of God's family, never cease to be the heirs of God's eternal kingdom.

FROM OBSESSION TO GIFT

My young friend Sheila discovered this gift of love as she journeyed away from a long and dangerous preoccupation during her teen years. She believed that food could be her friend only if she could control it. She asserted her control by purging herself of every bit of food she consumed. She was convinced that the process of eating and purging held the key to her security. For Sheila, this process promised purification and an avenue to safety and control. But her soul was lonely, and she was in great pain.

Finally, after years and years of this cycle, Sheila surrendered. She reached out of her cold loneliness toward God and discovered a love that would not reject her no matter what she had done or thought. She now finds herself in a world where she is known and blessed by God. In her gratitude she reaches out her hands every week, palms facing heaven, to receive the bread of life. Though the piece of bread is small, it is large enough to fill the corners of her soul, once occupied by self-hatred and darkness.

RECEIVING THE GIFT

When I place consecrated bread in people's hands, I wonder what they are thinking and feeling. I can tell a lot about their desire for this bread by how they hold their hands. Some grip their hands so tightly together that I have to poke the bread in between their fingers. Does this mean that their hearts are constricted and want only a thin shaft of love? I do not know. With other people, usually teenagers and young mothers, it takes me a moment to get their attention so that I can put the bread in their hands. Are they too distracted or self-conscious to give any time to God? I do not know. Many people bring their good manners with them to the altar and say, "thank you," when I put the bread in their hands. I wonder if their politeness is a way of keeping God at a dignified distance. My very favorites are the children who reach out, grab the bread, and quickly stuff it into their mouths. Oh, that they would always grab for God!

This bread that we come to take and eat is a wonderful gift, but it is not just a one-way gift. Having received this bread into our very being, we must not be content simply to take our satisfied selves home after church; we must share our renewed selves with the broken souls in our difficult world; we must reach out to those who have not been renewed by this bread. Fed as we are, we must now feed others. We have been given a world, and we have been given work to do in that world. Sustained by the bread we have taken and eaten, we have also been given enough love to accomplish that work.

BEN'S STORY

Ben was a businessman who gradually learned that God was calling him to respond to the gift of the bread of life. When he returned to church after years of staying away, he began to understand that this gift was not for him to keep. His response was not sufficient when he reached out and took the bread and ate it. For his action to be completed, he discovered that somehow he had to feed others. He had eaten many loaves before he knew what he was to do with all that bread alive within himself. He was to bring the love and compassion of the bread of heaven, with which he was now filled, to his business every day.

Originally, Ben had thought that he should volunteer in a soup kitchen or in an after school program downtown. But slowly he came to realize that while there would always be people to volunteer in important nonprofit missions, he might be the only person who was both willing and able to bring the light of love and truth to his own company. He believed that by being someone who was fed by justice and forgiveness, mercy and love, he could be most effective in the daily life of his business. Has he made a difference? He doesn't know. But he is convinced that if he hadn't chosen this path, life in the office would have been meaner, more thoughtless, tougher. He has never regretted his decision—and he never has stopped holding out his hands to be fed.

UNFULFILLED PROMISES

In cooking school, on television, and in magazines I see food raised to godlike status: I call this philosophy "salvation through sensation." The chef of the moment functions as a minister who promises to absolve us of all our ills by creating a masterpiece of flavor, design and expense. But, slacker that I am, I have never been able to recall, even just a few days after having enjoyed them, the wonderful flavors of these awesome meals. Salvation through sensation is fleeting.

Another philosophy that our culture seems to embrace, especially at the Thanksgiving holiday, is "salvation through satiety." One year, immediately before the Thanksgiving service at our church, I had to search through several large grocery stores for fruits and vegetables to fill our parish's cornucopia display. The grocery store aisles were packed with shoppers desperate to create "perfect" holiday meals. I could actually sense their anxiety. Seeking to recreate what they remembered of their childhood Thanksgiving dinners, and fearing that they might fail, they would be spending all day preparing a meal that would be consumed in a brief moment. And later, when they were full to the point of bursting, they would feel no real sense of satisfaction. In a sense, many of them would still be empty, still hungry.

FULFILLED PROMISE

Just a short time later I was standing at the altar in our church, looking out at our small congregation—here were people coming to be fed at God's table with a meal that always lives up to its promises. I looked at the bowed heads in front of me and knew that these gentle folk would receive food that would be forever fresh and would fill them. Like the gift of manna in the wilderness, the holy communion feeds us what we need for today. God gives us enough for today and will give us enough for tomorrow. We aren't overwhelmed with more than we can possibly eat today. There are no leftovers that will get lost in the back of the refrigerator. God's salvation is not accomplished through satiety.

Because the moment of communion is private, I will never know the motivations of the people in the congregation as they reach out their hands. In one of our eucharistic prayers, we pray that we will receive communion not for solace only, but for strength, and not for pardon only, but for renewal. Surely at different points in our lives, our reasons for receiving communion change. I will never know what the moment of communion means to a woman whose husband is about to leave her, or for someone who has just been awarded the promotion of his dreams but has yet to tell his family that they must move across the country. I will never know what it means even to the people who are as close to me as my next breath. I do know, however, that it is a privilege beyond comprehension to be the one who places that holy bread in all those upturned hands.

ALTAR BREAD

Many congregations use homemade bread for communion. If it is at all possible, they use a single loaf on the altar. When everyone partakes of the same loaf, there is a dimension of wholeness and equality; everyone is equally fed. A typical congregation needs only a few people to serve as bakers—a Bread Guild of about six people, each of whom is willing to bake twice a year, making enough bread for one month. If possible, involve children in the preparation; it is wonderful to see the magic in their young faces as a congregation is fed from the loaf the children made.

Some people are bothered that homemade bread is not as "tidy" as communion wafers. There are bound to be stray crumbs, even from a loaf that breaks cleanly. When my mother's parish began to use homemade bread, she found it enormously disturbing to see crumbs dropped on the carpet. So she bought the Altar Guild a cordless, handheld vacuum cleaner. To our amusement, everyone referred to it as the "ghost buster."

There are lots of recipes for altar bread. I have tried quite a few over the years, and I like the one that follows best. It is not a yeast bread; it is leavened with baking powder. You can easily double or triple the recipe. These loaves freeze very well for up to two months. I offer one word of caution: do not bake it too long.

This recipe makes bread that is quite similar to the altar bread used by the Society of Saint John the Evangelist at their monastery in Cambridge, Massachusetts and at Emery House, their retreat house in West Newbury, Massachusetts. My recipe calls for less flour. I like working with a moister dough, which yields a loaf that is easier to tear and distribute.

When the bread is handed to you at communion, look at it in your hands and know yourself to be in communion with generation upon countless generations of people who also have reached out their hands. And many of those people did so not even knowing why they were doing it. Be at one, even for a brief moment, with the richest and with the poorest, with the joyful and the devastated, and with all the faithful seekers who savor the taste of divine love in a tiny piece of bread. Next time, just before you pray for yourself, pray also for them.

Altar Bread
(Yield: depends on the size of the rounds]

1½ cups whole wheat flour

2 teaspoon baking powder

¼ cup honey

¼ cup cold water

¼ cup milk

2 tablespoons vegetable oil or olive oil

⅛ teaspoon salt

Preheat the oven to 400° F. Sift the flour and the baking powder together into a large bowl. Add all the remaining ingredients and stir with a wooden spoon. When the ingredients begin to pull together, use your hands. Knead the dough inside the bowl by folding it on itself and flattening it. Keep doing this until the ingredients are well incorporated. Pull off a piece of dough about the size of a golf ball and roll it into a ball. Using a rolling pin, roll it into a circle no more than one-quarter-inch thick. Try to make this disk as round and as neat as possible. Alternatively, you might roll out a larger amount of dough and trace or cut neat circles with a bowl or pot lid, four to eight inches in diameter, depending on your need. A four inch round will feed between twelve to sixteen people at communion, with a morsel large enough to taste and savor. And eight inch round will feed between sixteen and thirty-two.

Place the flat rounds of dough two inches apart onto a baking sheet covered with parchment paper. Using a sharp knife, cut a cross in the center of each round. Bake for eight minutes. Cool completely before wrapping in foil and storing in a plastic bag for freezing.

CHAPTER SEVEN

I magine sitting down to eat a meal under the setting Tuscan sun. The newly harvested fields have changed color—from green to pink to deep sienna. An excellent bottle of wine has been decanted at your table. You sigh with satisfaction and reach for the bread. But your taste buds register a strange taste; this Tuscan bread is peculiar. It has no salt.

Salt is a critical component of bread, regulating the kneading and enhancing flavor. But Tuscan bread is made with no salt. I once watched a young woman take a bite, frown, reach for the salt shaker, take another bite, scowl, and put down the rest of it in disgust.

But when Tuscan bread is paired with other foods—with soup, sauce, or beans—it tastes utterly different. All the salt it was "lacking" is supplied by the food. And the bread has its own contribution to make: it quietly and subtly supports and enhances the other foods, and the bowl of soup or sauce or beans is more delicious paired with the bread. The meal emerges as complete in a new way.

Tuscan bread looks very appealing as it comes out of the oven. The crust is hearty, the crumb is semi-dense, and the smell is deep and rich. Don't overlook its goodness just because the first taste is such a surprise. And it *is* a surprise. After taking my first bite, I looked at my husband and said, as if I had discovered a shocking truth, "This bread has no salt."

FAITH NEEDS NO SALT

It takes time to appreciate Tuscan bread; satisfaction is not instantaneous. Take the time to eat it slowly, feel its texture, and gather in its goodness. Time is its final ingredient. To eat and appreciate Tuscan bread, tear off a piece and smell it, close your eyes and really breathe in the depth of its richness. Now taste it. Chew slowly and taste beyond its saltlessness. Now use it for a sandwich, toast it, put it under an egg, or try one of the recipes in this chapter. And all things become new.

Once, as I sat munching on a piece of Tuscan bread and staring off into the horizon, I found myself wondering about faith. What could I intuit about faith by eating a piece of this unusual bread? For me, this bread is an icon that has led me from the abstract idea of faith to see a clearer vision of my Christian faith as an inherent reality.

LETTING FAITH GROW

First, let's consider the abstract idea of faith. Faith underpins all else; it is the lens through which you see and interpret life's daily mysteries. Faith in and of itself has infinite value. It unifies the fragmented experiences of our lives, showing us that there is a pattern to be discerned in them. Such faith may or may not have a religious component. That depends on our upbringing and our exposure to a particular tradition.

We enter life with a full capacity to be faithful. Think of the innocent and trusting nature of children. In an ideal world—in an ideal childhood, children begin the journey of faith by trusting their loving parents and being accepted in their extended families. Their parents and other adults bring them into a community of faith where they are taught the stories and traditions of that community's relationship with a loving God. Growing up with an increasingly sure sense of membership in the community, albeit with a necessary time of doubt and questioning, these children become young adults who adopt all or part of their community's values and beliefs.

I witnessed one especially joyous example of a little boy's journey in faith. His teacher in Vacation Bible School class, Brenda, had chosen Jesus' parable of the lost sheep. (Mt. 18:12-14; Lk. 15:3-7) She had cut out paper sheep and labeled each one with the name of a child in the class. When she finished telling the Bible story she sent the children into the hall to find their personal "lost sheep," which she had hidden there. It was a wonderful exercise made more wonderful by what happened next. She had forgotten one boy! Quickly, Brenda ushered the children back into the classroom and then ran for help. One of the grandmotherly helpers was pleased to respond to Brenda's urgent plea for someone who would cut out another sheep. Back in the classroom Brenda told the Bible story a second time, asking the little boy to sit next to her and play the part of the poor lost, heart-sore sheep that he was. At the end of the story, she again told him to go look in the hall. And there was a sheep with his name on it. He was found!

That morning the little boy discovered an essential lesson about the faithfulness of God. He learned to have faith in a God who would not lose him, no matter where he went. God would always know where he was and would want to have him near. I wish that all our children could know God's love so deeply.

Very few of us have lived an ideal childhood. Experience has taught me that most adults are burdened with false images of God and faith that have been with them since their earliest years. The nonverbal perception of God we carry within us is usually a reflection of the parent with whom we had the most difficulty. If your mother was short-tempered and prone to depression, your internal God might be joyless and impatient. If your father was loud and rough, your internal God might be boorish and harsh.

Misperceptions about faith also are rooted in early experiences of a parent's love. If you sensed that your parent's love was conditional and limited, then for you God's love may seem to be carefully apportioned. You may fear there will not be enough for you.

Or you might view God's love as judgmental and punitive. What does it mean to "have faith" in such a God? I remember a man who told me that he just didn't have enough faith. He couldn't sense depth, elasticity, or fortitude in his faith because when he was a child, neither his parents nor anyone else demonstrated faith in him. It took years of intentional spiritual discipline and participation in a community of faith before he could accept that God had had faith in him all along. He truly wanted to believe that God's love was merciful, forgiving and endless, but acceptance needed to come from within his deepest self, where it would override the negative messages from his childhood.

COMPANIONSHIP IN FAITH

To grow fully as children of God, we must mature in our faith as we mature in years. Children are self-centered little people, but adults understand that the world does not revolve around them and their needs. Yet in the journey of faith, many adults continue to ask "Do *I* have enough faith?" rather than "How is *God* faithful?" Our secular culture, I'm sorry to say, rewards individualism and fosters greed, both of which impede a faith journey.

The surest way to Christian maturity is to make the journey of faith in the company of faithful friends. Whether we find them in our church congregations or elsewhere, companions in faith play an important role when they talk with us, share with us, and pray with us about their own joys and confusions about living lives that are intentionally connected to God.

If we find ourselves all in a muddle, once again stewing in our insecurities, our companions can offer us a lifeline. Several years ago, I faced life-changing surgery, and in my fear, I was convinced that my faith wouldn't be sufficient to get me through. My companions prayed and laughed and cried for me, because in my fear, I was unable to do so. They imitated and demonstrated the faithfulness of God for me, in their own flesh. Through their love I was able to respond to this faithful God. In my response, I came to understand that we don't ever need to ask, "Do I have enough faith?" Faith simply *is*. It is unearned and unmerited, called forth by the faithfulness of God. As we mature, we become able to *live* this faith response.

In mature faith, we draw upon a history of responses to the faithfulness of God: not just particular instances of knowing God's love in our own lives, but also the centuries-long salvation history of the people of God. We become able, in some sense, to accept these events as our own history. God delivered *us* from slavery in Egypt; God was faithful in sending manna to feed *us* in the wilderness. Similarly, Jesus restored *our* sight when we were blind, and *we* stood in the crowd of 5,000 whom Jesus fed with five loaves and two small fish. Those collective memories are our eternal underpinnings, always with us, wherever we go. God's faithfulness is with us as we work each day; it is with us as we go to the altar on our wedding day; it is with us as we wait at the doctor's office; it is with us during our chemotherapy treatments; and it is with us when we stand over the new grave of our life's treasured partner. The history of past faithfulness steadies us, as a keel steadies a boat in rough waters.

THE GIFT OF TIME

When we understand that God's faithfulness always is with us, we must ask, "How will I respond to the faithfulness of God?" Here is where we exercise our free will; we may choose to fill our lives with so many external concerns that we leave no time to develop the faith that lies deep within us. We neglect to realize that time is one of God's greatest gifts.

In the last few years, "24/7" has become a part of our lexicon; I think of it as defining our human limitations. We have to live within the constraints of a fixed number of hours in every day. For that reason, I believe that in today's world, one of the greatest gifts we can give one another is our time. Living in the suburbs as I do, I am amazed each Saturday by the frantic pace of weekend suburban life. I observe people who have no thought for their need to be spiritually refreshed, whose pace of life permits no quiet time, no exploration of life's meaning. Instead, they fill their weekends with frantic running around: to stores, games, gyms, or parties. Years ago, I also ran with this crowd, commuting from my suburb into New York City. In the winter, I saw my town in daylight only on weekends. I know now that the spiritual cost of trying to live a 24/7 life is too high. I pray that some of my neighbors will stop running long enough to choose Sabbath time for their souls and bodies.

To give someone else a piece of our uninterrupted time is to give a gift of great value, a sure and concrete way to share our faith. As a parish priest, I am called to share my time. Simply spending time with people is one of the most significant ways I know to show them that they matter, that God loves them. I am not being asked to voice an opinion, fix something, or explain guidelines. A most effective way to mirror God's love for the souls in my care is to wait—wait for people to finish telling me a story, wait with them to finish a promised project, and wait with them to discover that they are sacred in God's sight. As I wait, I am mindful of Jesus' words in the Garden of Gethsemane: "Could you not keep awake one hour?" (Mk. 14:37)

Yet as much as I talk of the gifts to be discovered by patient waiting with others, I am not by nature a patient person. I still hate waiting for my birthday or for Christmas. Waiting for a phone call or for enough money to pay a bill is agony. At such times, I must work hard to take my own advice. I recall a time when I was forced to eat very slowly because of pain from nerve damage to a tooth. By slowing down, I ate less and enjoyed my food so much more. And I am reminded of my favorite scene from Alice

Walker's, *The Color Purple*: if people wait instead of rushing, they can see the color purple in the passing field.

COMPANIONSHIP IN CRISIS

Look at the people in your life. With whom do you spend your time? With whom do you wait? It is with these people that we live out our faith. The larger our circle, the greater the likelihood that we will experience times of crisis. When we choose to be a companion-in-waiting, seeing friends or family through a crisis, we are surely witnessing to God's faithfulness.

A hospital waiting room can be a lonely place at night. Once, my friend Jan waited through the night for the results of her husband's surgery. Not wanting her to be alone, I joined her for part of that long night. When I arrived at 3:00 a.m., I found her asleep. She stirred a bit but didn't appear to waken. Suddenly, however, she bolted awake as her overtired brain registered who I was. As we talked together, she told me that when I had first arrived she was vaguely aware of another person and thought how sad it was that someone else was waiting alone through the cold winter night. Only serious operations take place during these lonely hours, she thought, and realized that here was somebody else who needed companionship. Despite her exhaustion, she decided it was important to wake up fully and to be present for the other solitary person. With some surprise, then, she recognized that I had come to do that for her.

Times of great joy are also ripe for companionship. When we are together at such times, our faith in God is enlivened because we are participating in God's wonders. I was privileged to join with Bob's and Angela's family and friends at the home birth of their third child. Bob phoned me at midnight: "Come now. Tonight's the night." When I got to the house, all was in chaos: children crying, people trying to calm each other. Eventually, we settled into a routine, with the midwife tending to Angela while the rest of us kept busy with such tasks as putting the children to bed and washing dishes. Most people didn't stay through the night, but for those very few of us who remained, the long night witnessed good conversation and laughter, mixed with the singing of hymns and prayer. God's spirit blessed our time together, even the moments we passed just sitting around comparing our summertime pedicures. Finally, by candlelight and to the strains of old Baptist hymns, the waiting came to an end, and Isabel was born.

For me, the most precious waiting is with people who are crossing the bridge between this world and the next. Mary had been a faithful member of my neighborhood church, and the neighbors showed their deep affection by bringing food to her house during her final illness. On a Saturday afternoon, with the sounds of a televised football game in the background, we who were waiting took time out from our vigil by Mary's bed to eat lunch. There were not enough chairs for all of us to sit, so we sat on the floor and the stairs and leaned against walls. We ate our fill of the excellent food that had been made with such tenderness by loving friends who were also waiting—some with us and some not. It was amazing how in those difficult surroundings, the meal we shared became a feast. And we began to laugh, all of us—a son, a daughter, a grandchild, and a weary husband waiting to become a widower. Mary had always been a fastidious housewife. It seemed to us that she waited for us to tidy up: not until the food was gone and all the dishes had been washed did she take her last breath. After she had died, I gathered the family to commend her soul to God:

Into your hands O merciful Savior, we commend your servant Mary. Acknowledge, we humbly beseech you, a sheep of your own fold, a lamb of your own flock, a sinner of your own redeeming. Receive her into the arms of your mercy, into the blessed rest of everlasting peace, and into the glorious company of the saints in light. Amen.
(Book of Common Prayer, p. 465, Ministration at the Time of Death.)

As I look back on these and similar times of waiting, I realize that each such experience strengthens my faith. In some sense, these times of crisis are "out of the ordinary," but in another sense they are a part of the normal ebb and flow of the life of the human family. By choosing to be present, to set aside my own daily routine in order to support someone else who is in crisis, I am able to live my faith among the other members of my faith community. The crisis times let me glimpse God's indwelling presence in our midst and know how truly we are all "one in Christ."

SALT IS NOT NECESSARY

I think back to the young woman who rejected unsalted Tuscan bread because of its unfamiliar lack of flavor. In much the same way, many people think that their faith—and their life—needs to be saltier, needs to be expressed with more passion or more drama in order to be "real." The search for faith with salt can lead us to mistake emotionalism for truth. For example, it is easy to be seduced by an emotional experience of worship. Mature faith can be recognized not by how it makes us feel, but by how it makes us think and act.

Mature faith embraces the journey rather than the destination. It welcomes other travelers with whom we share our joys and pain along the way. The journey will bring us to understand that our faith is a gift of love from a loving God. When we know ourselves as God's beloved, our waiting will have been fruitful. Like Tuscan bread, our lives will sop up the good as well as the bad and make both into something new.

Tuscan Bread

(Yield: two loaves)

420 grams (4 cups) flour

250 grams (1 cup) water, at room temperature

140 grams (2 cup) levain

2 teaspoon active dry yeast

2 teaspoons salt, optional

When you measure the levain, be sure to reserve 200 grams (¾ cup) and feed it according to the instructions for Day Five. (See page 23.)

Combine all the ingredients in a mixing bowl or in the bowl of a heavy-duty mixer fitted with the dough hook. Running your mixer at the lowest speed, mix for one to two minutes. Alternatively, use a wooden spoon to mix manually by hand until all the ingredients have become incorporated, for about three to five minutes. On Speed 2, mix for another four to five minutes, or until the dough is shiny and soft. Or working manually, knead the dough on a lightly-floured surface for about six to ten minutes, adding flour as needed. Return the dough to the mixing bowl. For the first rising, place the bowl in a steam-filled microwave or cover it with a warm damp cloth and put it in a draft-free place. (See Hint 4, page 93.) The dough will not rise much during the first rising.

After the dough has been rising for one hour, place it directly on a lightly-floured surface. Degas the dough: Sprinkle flour on top of the dough and press down gently, releasing air. Fold the dough in half, bringing the top to the bottom. Press lightly and fold the dough in half from side to side, twice, pressing after each fold. Sprinkle a little flour in the bowl and return the dough to the bowl. Put it back in its rising place for the second rising, another forty-five minutes.

Dust two willow baskets lightly with flour or oil two nine-by-five-inch loaf pans. Pour the dough onto a well-floured surface and cut it into three equal pieces.

If you are using willow baskets, flour your hands and form each piece into a ball by pulling the top over the middle and sealing with your fingertips. Turn the dough one-quarter turn and repeat. Do this again. Now turn the dough so that the seam side is down. Cup your hands around the sides of the ball and a little under it. Roll the ball around a bit to seal the seam and to smooth the top. Now place each ball into its basket, seam side up. If you are going to be baking your loaves on a baking stone, put the stone on a rack in the lower third of the oven.

If you are baking in loaf pans, flour your hands and form each piece into a log just smaller than your pans: Form each piece into a rectangle about five inches wide and seven inches long. Fold the top down to just below the halfway point and pinch it sealed with your fingertips. Fold the bottom up to just above the halfway point and seal. Fold the top down so that it is even with the bottom and seal. With your hands cupped around the length of the log and slightly under it, rock the log back and forth to seal the seam and to smooth out the top slightly. Place each log in its pan with the seam side down.

Cover the dough-filled baskets or the pans with a cloth and set them on your counter, covered with a cloth, for the third rising. If you are planning to bake the free-form loaves one at a time, you may put one loaf in the refrigerator, still in its basket, tightly covered with plastic wrap. After twenty minutes, preheat the oven to 460° F and wait twenty minutes more. When the oven has reached baking temperature, add moisture by tossing in a tray of ice cubes or spraying water from a spray bottle. (See Hint 6, page 94.)

If you have used willow baskets, flour the baker's peel and tip one loaf from its basket onto the peel. (See Hint 7, page 94.) The dough might stick to the basket. If it does, gently pull if off and reform the ball on the peel by tucking the sides under. Score the top of the loaf by cutting a one-quarter-inch-deep cross with a sharp knife, razor blade, or lame. Slide the loaf onto the preheated baking stone in the oven. Bake for at least forty-five minutes. As soon as you put the first loaf into the oven, take the second loaf out of the refrigerator to begin its third rise. Remember to score the second loaf and to add a tray of ice cubes to the oven just before baking.

If you are baking in loaf pans, score each loaf with one lengthwise cut, one-quarter-inch deep, and bake the two loaves at once. Bake for at least forty-five minutes on a rack placed in the lower third of the oven.

This bread is done when the crust is dark brown, the top is hard, and it sounds hollow when you tap it. Remove your loaves from the oven (and from the loaf pans) and place them on a rack. Cool completely before slicing. Remember that bread continues to release moisture until it reaches room temperature.

Tuscan White Beans
(Yield: 4-6 servings)

app. 4 quarts vegetable stock (recipe follows)

1 pound large white kidney beans, soaked overnight

2 cloves garlic, minced

3 tablespoons parsley, chopped

1 sprig fresh sage

Salt

Pepper

The essence of this simple dish is found in its preparation time. Several hours of slow cooking makes this a savory treat. Although you could use canned beans, you'll find that starting with dry beans gives a far superior result.

Drain and rinse the beans, put them into a large pot, and cover with your own vegetable stock. Add the garlic, parsley, and sage to the beans and broth. Simmer for one to two hours or until the beans are the texture you want. Add salt and pepper to taste.

Vegetable Stock
(Yield: app. 4 quarts)

1 onion, coarsely chopped

3 stalks celery, chopped

3 cloves garlic, peeled and left whole

1 sprig fresh sage

3 tablespoons parsley, chopped

Place all the ingredients into a pot of at least one gallon capacity. Add four quarts of cold water. Bring to a boil, reduce the heat, and simmer for one-half hour. Strain the stock and discard the vegetables.

Tuscan Tomato Sauce
(Yield: enough for one pound of pasta)

2 pounds ripe tomatoes

Several cloves garlic, crushed

¼ cup extra virgin olive oil

2 cups red wine

Salt

Time is the key ingredient in this pasta sauce. I make it and can it in the fall, when the tomatoes are at their best, full of sunshine and rain. And when we eat this sauce during the cold winter months, we can taste and savor summer all over again. I prefer to use organic Roma tomatoes.

This recipe makes just enough for one meal, but if you have the time and the tomatoes are excellent, you could do an entire bushel, adjusting the quantities of other ingredients accordingly; a bushel of tomatoes would yield approximately twelve eight ounce jars of very rich sauce.

Peel the tomatoes by scoring the skins, dipping them briefly into boiling water, and plunging them into cold water to stop the cooking. The peels should slip off easily. Cut each tomato in half and remove the seeds. Put the tomatoes into a large pot. Add the garlic, olive oil, and red wine. Cover the pot and simmer. After several hours, uncover the pot and continue to simmer the sauce slowly until all that remains is a tomato paste. Add salt to taste.

If you've made a large quantity of sauce, you should have on hand canning jars and lids that you've sterilized according to the manufacturer's directions. Fill the jars and process them in a water bath for fifteen minutes. After the jars have cooled, store them in a dark, cool place.

This sauce is very rich. You need only enough to coat your pasta evenly. Remember not to overcook the pasta! Once the center is cooked soft, every additional moment of cooking is a moment of flavor and texture gone forever. Drain the pasta in a colander, warm the sauce in the pasta pot, reintroduce the pasta to heat with the sauce, and serve with good Parmesan cheese, salad, wine, and, of course, Tuscan bread.

CHAPTER EIGHT

I couldn't have been more shocked than when I learned that we students were to have a final exam at the French Culinary Institute. I had been having so much fun that I forgot that I was engaged in a professional educational experience. The exam was scheduled to last an entire day. There was going to be a written test covering such topics as the use of baker's percents, acidity of levain, and the gluten content of various grains, but we would spend the bulk of the day baking our own creations.

The baking assignment was very specific. Our breads must contain some kind of pre-fermented dough, such as levain; we were to justify our choice of shape, the scoring, and the baking temperature; we were to monitor and explain the temperature of the ingredients; and, finally, our loaves had to taste good! Luckily, we were given opportunities to ask questions of our instructor prior to the day of the final, and we were given time to experiment with ingredients in a "dry run."

Fears of failure and humiliation overwhelmed me. I had never before experienced such pre-exam panic. To create an original loaf of bread . . . one that had never been baked before . . . I was utterly awed by the task. From the depths of this awe, I began to think and dream about what I might create.

EXAM TIME AND THE
BREAD OF ABUNDANCE

ONE LOAF, MANY MEANINGS

I wanted my bread to reflect my abundant gratitude for all the discovery and joy that had brought me to this exam. My loaf, which would be sold just once at the school's own *boulangerie**, needed to be a ten-inch round composite of my gratitude and my rejoicing. Yes, I expected a lot from a single loaf of bread.

As the days went by, my classmates and I talked a little about how our ideas were forming. Some said they wanted their bread to be *nouvelle cuisine*, or funky New York style, or just plain easy to make. But there is little time for gossip in a production bakery that is operating at full tilt. And that is what our classroom had become during that final stage of our course. I found that it was hard for me to explain that I wanted my loaf to express not only my gratitude for new knowledge but also my thankfulness for God's abundant grace. My bread would honor God. I would create a tangible symbol of God's abundance out of ingredients mentioned—one way or another—in the Old Testament.

How would I assemble a loaf of abundance? Initially, I was tempted to include too many ingredients. I soon realized that a common misconception about abundance is that it implies quantity. But quantity and abundance actually have little to do with one another.

RECOGNIZING ABUNDANCE

True abundance is not suffocating wealth or too many cookies for the cookie jar. True abundance is having just enough and knowing it to be a blessing. Insisting on getting and holding onto more than enough is greed, and greed is the enemy of abundance.

In the same way, when we become convinced that we don't have enough, even the smallest shortfall can make us lose our vision of the heavenly Jerusalem. An obsessive desire can narrow our souls until we lose the ability to care for anyone but ourselves. In the grip of obsessions, we become self-absorbed; our compassion grows cold.

HEART ROT

I met a National Park Service ranger in the Maine woods one fall day when I was out hiking. His job was to cull damaged trees before winter set in. He told me he was looking specifically for spruce trees with "heart rot." Such trees are not obvious at first glance. Nevertheless, these trees are already dying. And although a fully dead tree can be expected to blow over in a winter storm, spruce trees with heart rot do not. They remain in place, twisting perilously in the wind. And because of their internal damage, their hearts rot. The ranger told me that to identify and remove the rotten trees "you've got to know your forest."

We may not twist in the winter wind as those trees do, but many of us know how it feels to live in the cold, dark absence of abundance. I think, for instance, of how easy it is to damage a relationship through anger and nastiness. It is sometimes frighteningly easy to devastate the person you love the most. There can be no abundance in the midst of betrayal; there can be only heart rot. I think also of obsessions that can keep us from living with abundance. In the grip of relentless debt, for instance, life may center on endless machinations to escape debt's clutches. We become more intimate with desperation than with hope. Trust dies. And there is no abundance in the midst of the scarcity of trust.

In my panic over my final exam, I found myself with a scarcity of trust. Perhaps the loaf itself could be the antidote I needed. I hoped to create a loaf that would truly be my bread of abundance.

CHOOSING BIBLICAL INGREDIENTS

The soul of my bread would depend on what went into it. I considered each ingredient carefully for its flavor, texture and color as well as for its proportion within the dough. The bread would rise and fall according to the percentage of each ingredient to the flour.

Flour—To represent the wholeness of the grain, I chose to use a mixture of white and whole wheat flours.

Water—Ever since the Spirit of God moved over the waters at the beginning of creation, water has been a symbol of birth and life. It purifies the earth and nourishes the food that grows from the ground. As Noah discovered when he found a renewed world beneath and beyond the mystery of the flood waters, water cleanses all sin.

Salt—Since the mind of God first conceived the seas, salt has been a part of creation, serving to both preserve and to purify. As a symbol of hospitality, salt welcomes the stranger. Yet Lot's wife was punished for her disobedience by being changed into a pillar of salt.

Yeast—An ancient and primal fungus, yeast serves to symbolize life breathed into lifelessness or the purification of the impure. I was delighted that our exam specifically required us to use some form of pre-fermented dough: the nomadic bakers of biblical times would have been in the habit of setting aside a handful of today's dough for use in tomorrow's loaf. I would use the levain I incorporate into all my breads to remind me of those ancient bakers.

Olive oil—In biblical times, some kind of oil was rubbed on people's faces as a visible sign of joy, gladness and balm. David wrote of this in Psalm 23, "you have anointed my head with oil, and my cup is running over." The kings of Israel and Judah were anointed with oil as a sign of their royalty.

Fruit of the vine—Unless they are first plumped in some liquid, raisins do not soften properly in bread dough. So I decided to simmer some raisins very briefly in red wine. I also needed to balance their sweetness and find a foil for their color and texture. Apricots seemed to offer a solution, but I could find no mention of apricots in the Old Testament. I asked friends for help. Find me apricots! And someone did. The New English Bible translation of the Song of Songs 2:5 reads, "He refreshed me with raisins, he revived me with apricots . . ."

Honey—Of course I had to include honey, a symbol of richness and abundance.

Spices—Finally, I decided to add a bit of cardamom as a background flavor. From a month spent in Jerusalem, I still cherished vivid memories of a city smelling of a mixture of cardamom and goat dung. I could recreate that memory by flavoring my loaf with a hint of cardamom and serving it with goat cheese.

This, then, was to be my bread of abundance. I chose each ingredient for a reason. Together, they would make up a whole. I would shape the dough into circular loaves to remind me of an infinite God, and I would score the sign of the cross on top of each. The loaves would honor God and celebrate all that was holy and sacred in my life as a baker.

A FLAWED BEGINNING

I nervously awaited the day set aside for our dry run, spending hours with a calculator, balancing ingredients and working the percentages. In my obsession, I desperately wanted to succeed; I wanted to be the best; I wanted to stand out. I forgot the vision of God's abundance; I wanted this to be about me. My pride and my greed were choking the very abundance that this bread was meant to honor.

On the day of our practice run, I measured and weighed, I macerated and chopped, I mixed and fermented, and I baked. Once the loaf had cooled, my instructor cut off a piece, tore it in two, and we both tasted. We looked at each other with equally sour faces. The bread was disgusting! This wasn't abundance. This bread honored no one and no thing. Overcome with worry and panic, I went back to the calculator to rework my percentages. As I sat at the computer late into the night, I imagined I could feel my heart rotting from too much self-absorption.

THE LEAP OF FAITH

But then grace came to me, and with it came the leap of faith: try this here and that there; omit one and add the other. That's when I knew I had devoted enough effort, enough ingredients, enough worry to this exam. My panic subsided, along with the selfishness.

Nervous but confident, I arrived at our kitchen on the morning of the exam and got to work. Again I measured and mixed, this time according to my new formula. Finally, at the very end of the day, we gathered around our instructor awaiting his evaluation of each of our creations. But his professional opinion no longer mattered to me. I knew that I could offer this loaf to God with joy: I had brought it into existence solely to be a sign of God's abundant delight in creation. The verdict? I heard his soft voice saying, "Now *this* is excellent."

Abundance is there for all of us. We can discover it in the oddest places—even in a loaf of bread at a New York City cooking school where I learned that true abundance doesn't make its home in the presence of worry, panic, or obsessive fixation on success through self-reliance. When I acknowledged my failure and began to rely on God, my faith prepared me to recognize and receive the gift of abundance. Abundance, like faith, was there all along, waiting for me claim it. After a dark and windy night wandering through the spruce trees I discovered abundance showing me the path and waiting for me to come home.

Bread of Abundance
(Yield: three loaves)

1,240 grams (7 to 8 cups) white flour

140 grams (1 cup) whole wheat flour

640 grams (2¼ cups) water at room temperature

4 teaspoons salt

3 teaspoons instant dry yeast

335 grams (1¼ cups) levain

80 grams (¼ cup) extra virgin olive oil

110 grams (⅓ cup) honey

½ teaspoons ground cardamom

140 grams (1 cup) raisins, boiled briefly in red wine to cover and drained

140 grams (1 cup) dried apricots, chopped

When you measure the levain, be sure to reserve 200 grams (¾ cup) and feed it according to the instructions for Day Five. (See page 23.)

Combine all the ingredients except the fruit in a mixing bowl or the bowl of a heavy-duty mixer fitted with the dough hook. Running your mixer at the lowest speed, mix for approximately two minutes. Alternatively, use a wooden spoon to mix manually until all the ingredients have become incorporated. Either way, add the raisins and apricots to the dough. On Speed 2, mix for another four to five minutes, or until the dough is shiny and satiny. Or working manually, knead the dough on a well-floured surface for six to ten minutes, adding flour as needed until the dough is soft but still shiny. Return the dough to the mixing bowl. For the first rising, place the bowl in a steam-filled microwave or cover it with a warm damp cloth and put it in a draft-free place. (See Hint 4, page 93) The dough will not rise much during the first rising.

After the dough has been rising for one hour, place it directly on a lightly-floured surface. Degas the dough: Sprinkle flour on top of the dough and press down gently, releasing air. Fold the dough in half, bringing the top to the bottom. Press lightly and fold the dough in half from side to side, twice, pressing after each fold. Sprinkle a little flour in the bowl and return the dough to the bowl. Put it back in its rising place for the second rising, about forty-five minutes.

Dust three willow baskets lightly with flour, or oil three nine-by-five-inch loaf pans. Pour the dough onto a well-floured surface and cut it into three equal pieces.

If you are using willow baskets, lightly flatten each piece of dough, pull two-thirds of it past the middle, and seal with your fingertips. Turn the dough one-quarter turn and repeat. Do this again. Now turn the dough so that the seam side is down. Cup your hands around the sides of the ball and a little under it. Roll the ball around a bit until the bottom is sealed and the top is without wrinkles. Place each ball into a basket, seam side up. If you are going to be baking these loaves on a baking stone, put the stone on a rack in the lower third of the oven.

If you are baking in loaf pans, flour your hands and form the three pieces into logs just smaller than your pans: Form each piece into a rectangle about five inches wide and seven inches long. Fold the top down to just below the halfway point and seal it with your fingertips. Fold the bottom up to just above the halfway point and seal. Fold the top down so that it is even with the bottom and seal. With your hands cupped around the length of the log and slightly under it, rock the log back and forth to seal the seam and to smooth out the top slightly. Place each loaf in its pan with the seam side down.

Cover the dough-filled baskets or pans with a cloth and set them on your counter for the third rising. After twenty minutes, preheat the oven to 460° F and wait twenty minutes more. When the oven has reached baking temperature, add moisture by tossing in a tray of ice cubes or spraying water from a spray bottle. (See Hint 6, page 94.)

If you have used willow baskets, flour the baker's peel and tip one loaf from its basket onto the peel. (See Hint 7, page 94.) The dough might stick to the basket. If it does, gently pull it off and reform the ball on the peel by tucking the sides under. Score the top by cutting a quarter-inch-deep cross into the loaf using a sharp knife, razor blade, or lame. Slide the loaf onto the preheated baking stone set in the oven. Bake for at least forty-five minutes. The remaining two loaves can stay in their baskets on the counter if your kitchen is cool. If the kitchen is quite warm, cover the third basket tightly with plastic wrap and place it in the refrigerator, returning it to the counter when you put the second loaf into the oven. Remember to score each loaf and to add a tray of ice cubes to the oven just before baking.

If you are baking in loaf pans, score the top of each loaf with a quarter-inch-deep cross and bake all three loaves at once. Bake for at least forty-five minutes on a rack placed in the lower third of the oven.

The bread is done when the crust is dark brown, the top is hard, and it sounds hollow when you tap it. Cool thoroughly on a rack.

This bread goes wonderfully with soup. Try it with black bean soup on a cold night. It will warm both your body and your soul.

Black Bean Soup

(Yield: 4-6 servings)

1 pound black beans, soaked overnight

2 cup cilantro, chopped

1 large green pepper

1 large onion

2 to 3 cloves garlic

3 tablespoons olive oil

Salt

Sour cream

Drain the beans and rinse them thoroughly. Place them in a large pot with enough salted cold water to cover. Add the cilantro. Bring to a boil and simmer for one hour, or until the beans are soft. Meanwhile, coarsely chop the green pepper, onion, and garlic. Heat the oil in a sauté pan, add the chopped vegetables and sauté them until the onion begins to caramelize. Set aside. When the beans are done, drain off and reserve at least half the cooking water. Combine the beans and the vegetables and puree them in a food processor or pass the mixture through a food mill. Gradually add enough of the reserved cooking water to the puree to achieve the consistency you want. Season to taste. Serve hot with a dollop of sour cream.

A meal of this soup and bread, along with some goat cheese, is truly a meal of abundance. Share it with someone who can't find the way out of the dark—a person who can't see the path through the forest on a cold and windy night. There is enough abundance here to remind even the most sorrowful person that God's world is a feast.

CHAPTER NINE

Y ou have taken the final loaf out of the oven, and it is cooling on your kitchen counter. Each loaf you've baked has served as a witness to your spiritual journey, your wandering along the pathways of God's surprises. What did you see along the way? Whom did you meet?

Maybe you met others who like yourself are not bakers but who also are trying to catch a glimpse of the divine hand in the corners of their lives. Or perhaps a long-lost companion has emerged from your memory—someone you hadn't thought of in years, someone who taught you about faith in God and God's faithfulness to you. When I bake, my thoughts often turn to Laurie, my closest childhood friend. We shared absolutely everything, and there were no secrets between us. We were *com-panions* in the literal sense of the word: we shared bread together. Laurie's favorite playtime snack was Wonder Bread slathered with butter. I remember she would "let" me hold the slick and slippery slices whenever she needed to free her hands. The memories of our companionship continue to bind us together even though we haven't seen each other in years.

When you look at your loaves on your counter top, you might recall the arduousness of your wanderings. There have been times when it seemed as though you had stumbled into a dense and dark forest that offered no clear way out. But just when your cry for help seemed to catch in your throat, you felt the hand of God lead you through the difficult passages. In gratitude, you savor the happy memories of kitchen warmth, the companionship of laughter, and the simple fun of having sticky dough all over your hands and arms.

SAVORING THE BREAD

It has been an adventure, and you are left with the lingering aroma of the baking bread. Even as it fades, though, you continue to feel its comfort. You know that at this moment you are as enveloped by God's mercy as you are by this gentle smell. To borrow an image from the title of a book by Rachel Field, you are as safe within this aroma as you would be if you were in "God's Pocket."

Look at your loaves cooling on your counter top. I hope you have discovered that there is nothing ordinary about your bread, just as there is nothing ordinary about the corners and edges of your life, which you once felt to be bereft of divine blessing. It is hard to look at your freshly baked loaves and not acknowledge that God is in the midst of all that is plain and ordinary.

All that's left now is to cut off a slice, dip it in olive oil or spread it with rich creamery butter, and savor each bite. It really does taste good, doesn't it? Earthy and crusty, even a little sour. Having been apart during the workday, my husband and I like to share a thick slice of bread at dinner when he comes home in the evening. Focusing on its texture and aroma, we break the slice in half, and we eat together. In this moment, we are aware of more than the goodness of the bread. We affirm that we are united, not just as husband and wife, but also in our deep and abiding trust in the goodness of our lives in God's sight.

Now it is your turn to break bread. Listen carefully for the voices of those calling out to you, "A thick slice, please, for me!" It is your turn to savor the bread, to feast with others, to trust in the pleasure and hope it will bring. And with the psalmist, to sing

Taste and see that the Lord is good; happy are they who trust in him!

(Ps. 34:8)

***Artisanal* bread** Free-form breads that are made in small quantity, not in vast production bakeries.

Autolyse (French) A method of mixing ingredients that bypasses the possibility of over-kneading dough. Ingredients are mixed briefly, covered, allowed to rest for up to one hour, mixed briefly again, and allowed to rest once more. Almost any dough can be mixed using this method.

Baker's Peel A flat, long-handled wooden or metal shovel used to transfer loaves into and out of the oven, especially free-form loaves that are being baked directly on the floor of the oven or on a stone.

Baking stone or pizza stone A flat, porous, ceramic surface, either square or round, that is placed in a conventional oven to mimic a brick oven and improve the crustiness of bread and pizza baked directly on it.

Biga (Italian) A fermented starter used in Italian breads. A mixture of yeast, flour, and water is allowed to rest at room temperature for an hour or more, until it ferments.

Boulanger (French) A bread baker.

Boulangerie (French) A bakeshop which sells bread.

Chef (French) Another word for levain, biga, or sourdough starter, sometimes referred to as "mother."

Crumb The soft, porous bread within the crust.

Degassing the dough The process of pressing air bubbles out of the rising dough. This process gives the yeast new food so that it may continue to work.

Gluten A protein found in wheat flour. When water is added to the flour, very thin strands of dough are created. The process of kneading pushes the yeast between the strands, giving the dough lift and flavor. Before kneading, the strands resemble a tangled head of hair. When the kneading is completed, the strands, now invisible, are as neat as newly combed hair.

Lame (French) A long-handled razor blade used for cutting shallow gashes in dough just prior to baking.

Levain (French) Fermented flour and water used to leaven dough. It imparts a slightly sour taste to the finished bread.

Willow or dough-rising baskets Round or oblong baskets which give a free-form, artisanal look to the finished bread.

1. Most bread recipes call for kneading the dough longer than is really necessary. If you have a heavy-duty mixer process the dough with the dough hook attachment for only four or five minutes after all the ingredients are well incorporated.Consider using a method the French call *autolyse,** which takes more time but prevents over kneading. Once all the ingredients are incorporated, allow the dough to sit in the mixer, covered with a towel, for 20 minutes. Then turn the mixer to medium for only a minute. Allow another 20-minute rest, and another minute of mixing.

2. I add about ¼ cup more liquid (water, olive oil, milk) than most recipes call for. It is better to have your dough moister rather than drier, even though it will be more difficult to handle.

3. Don't forget the salt. If you do, call your loaf Tuscan Bread (see Chapter 7).

4. To create a warm, humid environment for dough fermentation (rising), put a glass measuring cup full of water in a microwave and boil the water. Then, leaving the cup of water in the microwave, place the uncovered bowl of dough in the microwave during its rising time. While you are degassing the dough (punching it down) to prepare it for the second rise, bring the water back up to a boil.

5. If you are making more than one loaf and your oven can accommodate only one loaf at a time, place other loaves in the refrigerator, covered tightly with plastic

wrap. You can even leave them in the refrigerator overnight, but remember to bring the dough up to room temperature before baking.

6. Just before baking the loaf toss a tray of ice cubes into the oven. Of all the ways I have tried for adding steam to the baking process, this one works the best. It sounds wonderful, and kids will love it. But if you have an electric oven with a heating coil that could be cracked by the sudden cold, use a spray bottle of water instead. Spray the inside walls of the oven, wait two minutes, and spray again.

7. To use a baker's peel to transfer a free-formed loaf of bread onto a baking stone in the oven: first dust the peel with flour and then tip the formed dough onto it as close to the front edge as possible. Place the front edge of the peel on the center of the baking stone and push a little bit forward quickly, then pull it back quickly in a sort of stuttering motion, leaving the loaf behind.

8. Bake the loaf longer and at a higher temperature than most recipes say. The crust should be a very deep brown and hard, and the loaf should sound hollow when you tap it. I bake almost all my levain-based breads at 460° for at least 40 minutes.

9. Cool completely before slicing. Bread continues to release moisture until it reaches room temperature.

10. Bread freezes nicely when tightly wrapped. But don't leave it in the freezer longer than two months. After that it begins to taste like the freezer.

Most chain grocery stores have just about everything any home baker needs to bake wonderful bread. For specialized items, I shop online at the following web sites:

The Baker's Catalogue
P. O. Box 876
Norwich VT05055
1-800-827-6836
www.bakerscatalogue.com and www.kingarthurflour.com

A comprehensive source for everything from King Arthur Flour and yeast to equipment such as dough-rising baskets, baker's stones and peels, professional-grade loaf pans, and kitchen scales—as well as almost any other baking item your heart could desire.

Williams-Sonoma
1-800-541-2233
www.williams-sonoma.com

This high-end source for cooking supplies and equipment offers an extensive array of baking equipment.

Amazon.com
www.amazon.com

Not just an online bookstore, Amazon also stocks competitively priced heavy-duty mixers.

The Bread Bakers Guild of America
www.bbga.org

This site incorporates links to merchandise, books, and more. You can find anything you want to know about bread baking. There is also continuously updated information about Team USA, a bread-baking team that competes in an international competition in Paris.

The French Culinary Institute (New York City)
1-888-FCI-CHEF
www.frenchculinary.com

Check this site for details about the Art of International Bread Baking, the course that taught me so much.

Beard, James A. *Beard on Bread*. New York: Knopf, 1995.

Curry, Rick, S.J. *The Secrets of Jesuit Breadmaking*. New York: HarperCollins, 1995.

Hensperger, Beth. *Baking Bread: Old and New Traditions*. San Francisco: Chronicle Books, 1992.

Jaine, Tom. *Baking Bread at Home: Traditional Recipes from Around the World*. New York: Rizzoli, 1996.

The King Arthur Flour 200th Anniversary Cookbook. Woodstock, Vt: Countryman Press, 1990.

Leader, Daniel and Judith Blahnik. *Bread Alone.* New York: William Morrow, 1993.

Reinhart, Peter. *Brother Juniper's Bread Book: Slow Rise as Method and Metaphor*. Reading, MA: Addison-Wesley Publishing Company, 1991.

——— *Crust and Crumb*. Berkeley: Ten Speed Press, 1998.

INDEX TO RECIPES